W9-ALL-127

THE
BATTLE OF
BUNKER'S HILL

by John R. Elting

Foreword by Harold L. Peterson

PHILIP FRENEAU PRESS

Monmouth Beach N. J.
1975

Other titles in the Philip Freneau Press
Bicentennial Series on the American Revolution

AMERICAN MAPS AND MAP MAKERS OF
THE REVOLUTION
Peter J. Guthorn
LC No. 66-30330/ISBN 0-912480-02-5

BRITISH MAPS OF THE AMERICAN REVOLUTION
Peter J. Guthorn
LC No. 72-79889/ISBN 0-912480-07-6

THE HESSIAN VIEW OF AMERICA 1776-1783
Ernst Kipping
LC No. 72-161384/ISBN 0-912480-06-8

AT GENERAL HOWE'S SIDE 1776-1778
Ernst Kipping
LC No. 73-94002/ISBN 0-912480-09-2

VALLEY FORGE CRUCIBLE OF VICTORY
John F. Reed
LC No. 70-76769/ISBN 0-912480-04-1

THE BATTLE OF TRENTON
Samuel S. Smith
LC No. 65-28860/ISBN 0-912480-01-7

THE BATTLE OF PRINCETON
Samuel S. Smith
LC No. 67-31149/ISBN 0-912480-03-3

FIGHT FOR THE DELAWARE 1777
Samuel S. Smith
LC No. 74-130878/ISBN 0-912480-05-X

THE BATTLE OF MONMOUTH
Samuel S. Smith
LC No. 64-56379/ISBN 0-912480-00-9

This Bicentennial Series
on the American Revolution
has been designed throughout by Paul R. Smith

Photography by Daniel I. Hennessey.

Copyright 1975 by Philip Freneau Press
Library of Congress No. 75-3540
International Standard Book No. 0-912480-11-4

FOREWORD

Every student of the American Revolution should be thoroughly familiar with the Battle of Bunker's Hill. Its importance can hardly be overestimated. It was the first major battle of the war. True, American Minutemen had charged a detachment of British Regulars at the North Bridge in Concord, but at Lexington the Americans had been dispersing when the shooting started and most of the Lexington/Concord affair had involved less formal harrassing tactics. Bunker's Hill showed whether Americans could face ferocious assaults by professional soldiers and hold their ground. A large number of them could, and this provided a lesson for both sides as well as a great stimulus to Colonial confidence. The whole battle from planning to conclusion also tested leadership and organizational skills for all officers involved, and the findings brought radical shifts in both armies. Ideas changed along with personnel. High ranking officers in each army found themselves relegated to insignificant posts. Some never commanded troops in important actions again. Others were catapulted to prominence. Of the British officers present, three, Howe, Clinton and Burgoyne, went on to command armies while their commander, Gage, went home in semi-disgrace. On the American side only Nathanael Greene rose to the first rank during the war and he had been on its periphery. Others, such as John Stark, a key figure in the battle, played important if lesser roles in the coming years.

Despite the obvious significance of this battle, most Americans know it only in myths. They have been nurtured on stories of three ill-advised and suicidal assaults by heavily encumbered British troops laboring uphill against entrenched Americans who picked them off easily until their ammunition ran out, and then were forced to retreat because they did not have bayonets.

Actually Bunker's Hill was a much more complicated battle. There were mistakes on both sides, sins of omission and commission. Given the situation, and the understanding of it by field commanders, the British plan of attack made sense. It was not the mindless series of assaults that has been claimed. The plans did not work as conceived for a number of reasons, but few battle plans do, even when the terrain and the enemy's troop dispositions are better known than they were on June 17, 1775. The British soldiers were not unduly burdened, and there was a reason for the equipment they did carry. The Americans did experience a lack of ammunition, but they were not completely without it when the British finally scaled the redoubt.

Until now it has not been easy for a student to obtain the true story of Bunker's Hill. Many of the facts have lain buried in scattered primary sources, hard to locate and put together. Few of the professional historians who have written about the battle have had the necessary military background to evaluate the situation and assess the alternatives available to the opposing leaders. Colonel John Elting is both a trained scholar and a professional soldier, who has had personal experience with military joint planning. In this volume he brings both disciplines together and focuses them on this crucial engagement. Also he expands the coverage to include all phases of the military and naval actions, providing new insights and analyses as well as previously unpublished facts. It is an achievement that deserves the thanks of all who are interested in American military history or the Revolution in general.

Harold L. Peterson
Chief Curator, National Park Service

CHAPTER I
THE HOSTILE SHORE

BUNKER'S HILL IN A NUT SHELL

"Friday, 16th. Our men went to Charlestown and intrenched on a hill beyond Bunker's Hill . . .
Saturday, 17th. The Regulars landed a number of troops and we engaged them. They drove us off the hill, and burnt Charlestown. Dr. Warren was lost in the battle, the siege lasted about three hours . . ."

Paul Lunt's Diary, May—December, 1775[1]

England was far away. On favorable winds, a fast, well-handled ship might make the crossing to North America in four to six weeks, but the average voyage consumed between two and three months.[2] Lumbering convoys of transports and supply ships sometimes required even longer. Storms might scatter whole fleets, or unfavorable winds hold them penned in English harbors while cargoes spoiled and passengers sickened. Well-considered orders out of London might prove hopelessly out-of-date when opened in Quebec or Boston. A British commander in North America must have the courage to act on his own responsibility—always under the knowledge that he risked England's hold on North America, and his own career.

Imperial Great Britain and its American colonies stumbled into a generally unwanted collision at Boston in 1774, when the British Parliament resolved to make an example of that city for its famous "Tea Party." Since Boston was the major fountainhead of American obstreperousness toward British rule, its reduction to proper obedience was a justifiable political objective. This political decision, however, begot a most unattractive assortment of military problems.

Boston lay behind a fanged screen of reefs and ledges. "It is a safe and pleasant Harbour within, having but one common and safe enterance, and that not very broad, there scarce being roome for 3 ships to come in board and board at a time; but being once within, there is anchorage for 500 Ships. This Harbour is made by a great company of Islands, whose high Cliffs shoulder out the boistrous Seas, yet may easily deceive any unskilfull Pilote; presenting many faire openings and broad sounds, which afford too shallow waters for any Ships, though navigable for small boats . . ."[3] The inner harbor was comparatively shallow, edged with tidal islands, salt marshes, and broad mud flats, all laced with obscure and tricky little channels known only to local residents. Harbor currents varied with the tides and seasons; winter storms and fogs doubled the hazards.

The Royal Navy had trouble with Boston harbor. Arriving in late 1774, the 64-gun *Asia*—considerably smaller than the standard 74-gun line-of-battle-ship—had to wait for the spring tides to get up into the inner harbor.[4] The 20-gun *Glasgow* sloop-of-war, fresh from a complete refitting at the Halifax naval yard, went on the rocks off Nantasket and lost her rudder: With Boston's limited facilities, she was not completely repaired until the next spring.[5] In May 1775, the 4-gun schooner *Diana* (See Chapter VI) was lost when the ebbing tide left her aground off Noddle's Island during a minor squabble at the north end of the harbor.[6] Other British warships were noted as running aground, with various degrees of damage as long as the English held Boston.[7] But Boston harbor's dangers were neutral: When Admiral D'Estaing's battered French fleet put in to refit during the autumn of

1778, its great line-of-battle-ships had to anchor in the outer harbor—and an American pilot wrecked the 74-gun *Magnifique* while bringing her in.[8]

The topography of this whole Dorchester-Boston-Charlestown area has changed completely since the Revolution, its energetic citizens having uprooted their hills to fill in the surrounding swamps and mud flats. In 1775 Boston itself was a hilly area with several heights (of which much beshaven Beacon Hill is the only remainder) that were visible well out to sea. The seaward approaches to its inner harbor were protected by the powerful island fortress of Castle William.[9] However, Castle William, and also the entire inner harbor, were dominated by the hills of the Dorchester Peninsula, south of Boston. Heavy enemy artillery emplaced on these Dorchester Heights could make Boston a trap. General George Washington's construction of batteries there forced the British to evacuate Boston hurriedly in March 1776.

In much the same way, Breed's Hill on the Charlestown Peninsula commanded the northern end of Boston and the narrow passage into the "Back Bay" (west of Boston) and the Charles River.

Consequently, if the British wished to establish a secure beachhead around Boston, they would have to hold both the Dorchester and Charlestown peninsulas, and maintain a naval force in Boston harbor capable of dominating its many islands and minor channels. Both of those peninsulas, as well as the Boston Peninsula itself, were connected to the mainland by narrow "Necks" which could be easily blocked by fortifications, and thereafter held by relatively small garrisons.[10] All communication between the forces occupying the three peninsulas would have to be by water; the troops on Dorchester Peninsula would be comparatively isolated in bad weather. The Dorchester area had few inhabitants, and Charlestown soon was evacuated (see Chapter VI), so that there would be no local opposition. Boston, however, remained a problem.

Boston was a hard-knuckled, independent-minded seaport community. In 1775, with a population of approximately 16,000, it was the third-largest town in British North America. Its merchants and seafarers were men accustomed to hazard: Smuggling, illicit trade with enemies in time of war, and privateering—which might verge on plain piracy—were accepted occupations.[11] Periodic bare-knuckle clashes between its South and North "enders" were common. In their own way, most Bostonians held to a rigid Puritanism; religion was a central feature of their lives, and religious controversy a serious matter. Doctrinal disputes within one congregation ended with the dissident occupants of the gallery relieving themselves on the heads of their brethern on the floor below—then going forth to commission themselves a handsome new church of their own.[12] Amid such religiosity, liquor was plentiful, cheap (" ..a man may get drunk for a copper or two."), and often bad; British officers feared it would be deadlier than the Yankees.[13] Theaters, however, were not permitted—"No such thing as a play house, they were too puritanical a set to admit of such lewd Diversions, tho' ther's perhaps no town of its size cou'd turn out more whores than this cou'd."[14] Some Americans blamed this last condition on the presence of licentious soldiery, but—long before British troops arrived—one of Boston's largest hills was famous locally as "Mount Whoredom."[15] After all, Boston was a seaport, and sailors always have preferred basic physical pleasures to church-going.

Whatever their pleasures and prejudices, Bostonians intended to manage their own lives. During the crisis years of 1768-1770, they had crowded a British garrison out of their town by clever, unrelenting exploitation of the hesitations of English officialdom, and insistence on their own rights as free Englishmen—plus an increasing use of raw force that culminated in the so-called "Boston Massacre." They were no more docile in 1774, if slightly more prudent: England might be determined to punish them, yet they knew from past experience that Lieutenant General Thomas Gage, the British commander in North America, would be most reluctant to use force.[16] They therefore set about hampering his operations in every way.

The Boston Selectmen made difficulties about supplying quarters for the troops. They persuaded Gage to station guards over their brickworks, which their unpaid laborers were threatening to damage—then refused to sell him any bricks. Sentries were heckled; a corporal who went to a sentry's assistance was charged with having abused a citizen. Gage's request that the troops be allowed to use Faneuil Hall for divine services was rejected.[17] Lieutenant Jeremy Lister of the 10th Regiment of Foot arrived that November from a tiny post on Lake Erie where he had been ". . commanding officer, Judge, and Justice.": Boston greeted his regiment with curses and "dirt."[18] The town watch was zealous in apprehending soldiers who might be considered as disturbing the slumbers of respectable citizens, and used its halberds freely on officers and enlisted men alike to enforce its orders.[19]

There was no cringing. Heaviest of the punishments Parliament visited on Boston was to close its port to all merchant shipping. This destroyed the town's major industry: Thousands of sailors, shipyard workers, warehousemen, and clerks were abruptly out of work. Had it not been for food sent overland from the other colonies, many of them would have faced starvation. Yet these hungry men refused work offered by the British occupation forces, greatly slowing the construction of barracks and the maintenance of British shipping. Everything the English did was watched, and reported inland to Massachusetts authorities. Weapons were stolen and smuggled out of town. Soldiers were urged to desert ". . either Singly or in Companys . . .," and given all possible assistance when they did so.[20]

Gage endured this semi-passive resistance with amazing patience, even to granting the Selectmen's demand that off-duty soldiers be forbidden to wear their sidearms—a deprivation that left them at a decided disadvantage in back-alley brawls with the inhabitants.[21] In part, such permissiveness was natural to Gage, but he also was troubled by the knowledge that many of these Americans owned weapons and might—given the right opportunity—break out in armed revolt. There were rumors of such planned uprisings, and of a plot to murder British officers.[22] On one occasion Gage was crowded too far: He even had allowed a ceremony commemorating the anniversary of the Boston Massacre, but jerked the Selectmen up short when they proposed to cap it by a torchlight procession that night.[23]

Behind sullen Boston lay Massachusetts, by tradition and fact the most recalcitrant and military of England's American colonies. By late 1774, Gage was certain of both its opposition and its ability to suddenly muster thousands of militia. Though British officers might ridicule the efficiency of such troops, their numbers were impressive. In September 1774, serious Hugh, Earl Percy, Colonel of the 5th Regiment of Foot and no admirer of Americans, conceded "What makes an insurrection here always more formidable than in other places, is that there is a law in this Province, Wh' obliges every inhabitant to be furnished with a firelock, bayonet, pretty considerable quantity of ammunition . . . They are, moreover, trained four times in each year, so that they do not make a despicable *appearance* as soldiers . . ."[24]

To many British officers, their principal military problem was

4

the fact that Boston was a dead end. Its only real military value lay in its harbor which—for all of its difficulties—was one of the best in America. But any advance inland from Boston would have to move through ". . a country wh' is so penetrated by hills, woods, & ravines, as makes it the most favorable spot in the world for the irregular, undisciplined troops of the rebels."[25] It would be difficult to supply such an advance: Gage's army had few wagons and teams; the Charles and Mystic rivers, which emptied into Boston harbor, were too shallow for large warships and transports. Worst of all, there was no logical objective—the capture or destruction of which would cripple the American rebellion—for such an offensive.

Meanwhile, with practically all the British troops in North America concentrated in Boston, the growing revolt was spreading unchecked throughout the colonies. Unless the Americans could be brought to battle near Boston and thoroughly crushed, the American rebellion was likely to grow into a major war.

CHAPTER II
THE NONCHALANT GENERAL

Thomas Gage, so his friend Dr. Richard Huck regretfully concluded in 1759, had ". . too much Nonchalance." Huck had come to North America as a military physician three years earlier; thereafter, he followed the drums through defeat and victory to the final conquest of French Canada. A man of incisive wit, his letters remain an unofficial history of those campaigns. And in that phrase, ". . too much Nonchalance," he caught one major reason why another British army would bleed so sorely, years later, at a place named Bunker's Hill.[1]

This Thomas Gage was a younger son of aristocratic lineage but straitened fortune. He had come into the British Army young, had known defeat at Fontenoy in 1745 during the War of the Austrian Succession, and victory of a sort in the Scottish Highlands under the Duke of Cumberland the next year. By 1755, when the beginnings of the Seven Years' War brought him to Virginia, he had become lieutenant colonel of the 44th Regiment of Foot through the normal English methods of preference and purchase.[2] The final day of Major General Edward Braddock's expedition against Fort Duquesne saw him leading the British advance party through the open woods beyond the Monongahela fords—into sudden collision with advancing French and Indians. What really happened in that howling, deadly confusion never can be known; Gage came out of it with two slight wounds and some questioning of his ability and courage.[3]

Through the next year, however, he worked effectively to restore discipline in his shaken regiment. John Campbell, Earl of Loudoun, the new British commander in America considered him ". . . a good officer [who] keeps up Discipline strictly." This approval furnished Gage a major opportunity: The methodical, long-headed Loudoun was concerned with training his troops in the art of wilderness fighting, and in securing qualified irregulars to scout and screen for them. Indians were undependable, American rangers expensive and undisciplined. For years Gage had sought promotion to the then lucrative grade of colonel without success: In December 1757 he offered to raise a regiment of light infantry at his own expense, himself to be its colonel. Loudoun approved and gave him every help. In their plain brown uniforms and special light-weight equipment, "Gage's Chasseurs"—officially, the "80th Regiment of Light-Armed Foot"—were the first regular light infantry regiment in the British Army. Properly officered, trained, and employed, they could have been thoroughly effective. But, aside from his colonel's prerequisites, Gage showed little further interest in them.[4]

For Major General James Abercromby's carefully prepared 1758 campaign against Fort Ticonderoga, Gage was appointed a brigadier and third in command. He had served in North America for three years, but it was the second in command—the recently arrived and quickly beloved George Howe—who saw that the army was reequipped and trained for forest warfare. When Howe was killed in an advance-guard squabble, Gage did not fill his boots. The British offensive fell into confusion; Abercromby threw his regulars away in a blind frontal attack on the French fortifications, and fled. Somehow, no account of the battle mentions Gage.[5]

In 1759, Gage's personal friend, Major General Jeffrey Amherst, led the British. Gage, fresh from marriage to a beautiful American heiress, was given the mission of capturing the French post of La Galette on the Saint Lawrence River, while Major General James Wolfe struck at Quebec, Colonel John Prideaux attacked Fort Niagara, and Amherst himself advanced up Lake Champlain. The other columns seized their objectives, but Gage hesitated; eventually, he declared his task impossible and would not risk even a reconnaissance in force. For the rest of the war he commanded the rear elements of Amherst's renewed advance.

He did this very well, being a good administrator. The fighting done, he governed the Montreal district for three years with great success. In 1761, in the general promotions to celebrate the end of French resistance in America, he was made a permanent major general. When Amherst was recalled to England in late 1763, Gage—the next senior officer—succeeded him as the British commander in chief in North America.

His problems were complex and increasing—friction between royal governors and local troop commanders, between aggressive settlers and Indians, and between the colonies. The Stamp Act sparked clashes between citizens and troops, which came to a head with the Boston "Massacre." Through it all, Gage remained tactful, careful, modest, and understanding. He was honest with official funds, strict with corrupt or disorderly subordinates, attentive to the good of the service, popular with his fellow officers and most Americans. A loyalist newspaper, *Rivington's New York Gazetteer,* would refer to him as ". . this most valuable and sincerely beloved personage . . ."[7] If his relations with certain rough-barked characters—such as irascible Colonel John Bradstreet and Major Robert Rogers, late of the Rangers—hinted that a certain petty meanness might lurk behind Gage's pleasant manners, these were passing irritations.[8] By 1773, events had quieted enough for him to return to England on leave.

The Boston "Tea Party" broke in abruptly on his rest. He was consulted as an expert on America, and—in a most uncharacteristic flourish—informed King George III that he could bring Boston to heel with four regiments.[9] Taking him at his word, the British government sent him back as a lieutenant general, Commander in Chief of His Majesty's forces in the American Colonies, and Governor and Vice Admiral of and in Massachusetts. In theory, his power was almost absolute: In practice, it was all mist and moonshine. Massachusetts received him politely; then disobeyed or ignored him, governing itself through an improvised Provincial Congress. Worse, it began preparing for war. Other New England colonies followed its example, and there was growing sympathy throughout North America. In late August 1774 Gage abandoned his exposed headquarters at Salem, and retired into Boston; early in September he began fortifying the narrow Neck which was the only land approach to that town. Besides the four regiments (see chapter V) sent from England and Ireland, he called in most of the British troops in outlying North American garrisons. His letters and reports turned pessimistic: All New England must be occupied, and not less than 20,000 men would be required. But this correspondence held little urgency: These were measures "you" in England should consider; the King and his ministers must decide what, if anything, was to be done. Meanwhile, he would avoid "any bloody Crisis" as long as possible.[10]

To achieve this, he held his troops under tight and sometimes savage discipline. When brawls broke out between soldiers and civilians, the soldier frequently was the only one punished, regardless of actual guilt. Armed Americans were allowed to come and go through the slowly building fortifications on the Neck; nothing effective was done to stop the constant smuggling of arms and ammunition out of Boston.[11] When enlisted men of the 47th Foot tarred and feathered a "countryman" who was attempting to buy weapons from a soldier, Gage "much disapproved."[12] The net result was that discipline suffered and morale declined. A good many officers came to consider Gage a mere ". . Tommy [who] feels no affection for his Army."[13] Also, they worried over Gage's nonchalant indifference to military matters. The fortification of the Boston Neck was postponed several times because of rain; the guards there and at the magazine had no positive orders until late December; no orders for possible emergencies were published until the 30th of that month. It was 8 January 1775 before Gage thought of ordering any reconnaissance and mapping of the roads running inland from Boston—and 22 February before two officers were selected and given orders.[14] By then the weather was savage, and the temper of the areas through which they must work was equally hostile.[15] In England there was anger over Gage's temporizing, and distress concerning the limited information he furnished. The Earl of Dartmouth, Secretary of State for the Colonies, prodded him, with little success.[16] In one thing only, and that far from Boston, was Gage energetic: He had personal knowledge of Indian warfare, yet he urged Canadian and frontier authorities to raise the tribes against the Americans, and considered promoting slave rebellions in the southern colonies.[17]

Eventually, under emphatic urging from England, Gage assayed decisive action.[18] The result was the fiasco of 19 April at Lexington and Concord. It was poorly planned and poorly executed: Orders were mislaid, troop movements dangerously delayed. Finally Percy dexterously extricated the almost-overwhelmed expedition, by way of the Charlestown Peninsula, halting on Bunker's and Breed's hills across the channel from Boston. A brigade was landed to reinforce him, and began to fortify the narrow western approach to Bunker's Hill.[19]

At this hour, Admiral Graves, the British naval commander, gave Gage a harshly realistic recommendation: Clear the approaches to Boston by burning Charlestown and Roxbury and fortifying Bunker's Hill and Roxbury Heights. Gage objected that his army was now too weak. Graves offered to put all of his marines ashore, and provide enough seamen to man Castle William so that Gage could use the 64th Foot, then in garrison there. His warships would keep Boston in subjugation by the threat of bombardment. Such prompt, aggressive action would give the English a secure beachhead. Gage declined, and tumbled his troops back into Boston. Seizing Roxbury well might have been a bloody business, requiring determination and tactical skills Gage never displayed. But there is no sensible explanation for his evacuation of the already half-fortified Charlestown Peninsula.[20]

Gage would only ask again for 20,000 men—which England would need another year to raise or hire in Germany—and lament. "In our present state all warlike preparations are wanting. No survey of the adjacent country, no proper boats for landing troops, not a sufficient number of horses for the artillery or for regimental baggage. No forage, either hay or corn of any consequence—no waggons or harness for horses, except some prepared by Colonel Cleveland for the artillery.

"No fascines or pickets. The military chest att the lowest ebb . . . The rebellious colonys will supply nothing . . . Flat bottomed boats are much wanted . . . Very few or no spies; we are therefore intirely ignorant of what they are about in the neighborhood. . ."[21]

Gage had held supreme command in North America for almost a year, yet nothing in these complaints admitted that he could be in the least to blame for the uncomfortable military position they portray. He still would be in supreme command during the battle of Bunker's Hill.[22]

CHAPTER III
THE FRUSTRATED GENERAL

Samuel Graves, Vice Admiral of the Blue, commanded from Nova Scotia southward to "The Floridas."[1] His missions were many—enforce the closure of Boston Harbor, prevent smuggling and trade in contraband goods, halt all importation of arms and ammunition into the American colonies, uphold the authority of the British government, and extend all possible aid to loyal subjects and their property. His most pressing responsibility was the support of General Thomas Gage's army in and around Boston. His various orders did not, however, include instructions as to what his conduct should be in case the ". . Provincials . . . proceed to Acts of Violence against His Majesty's Forces by sea or land."[2]

Graves was an English admiral of his day, insistent on the prerequisites of his grade and station, eager to push his nephews' careers, loudly abusive when crossed. British Army officers in Boston generally disliked him.[3] They were delighted with "A curious event . . . Our Admiral has been boxing in the Street with one of the Commissioners of the Customs [and] has had the worst of it . . ."[4] What these officers never comprehended was that Graves also was a competent naval officer who gave General Gage unstinting support and sound advice.[5] Though reluctant to take forcible action in the absence of any positive orders, he was quicker than Gage to meet emergencies and far readier to fight.

Gage's army was totally dependent on Graves' squadron. After the Lexington/Concord fight, it could obtain neither food nor firewood from its usual sources in New England. It could not advance out of Boston—except across the narrow Boston Neck—without naval assistance; information as to what was happening elsewhere in North America could come only by sea. In short, by itself, the Boston garrison had scarcely more mobility than a marine landing detachment. It controlled only the ground it occupied, knew little more than its spies and sentries could report, and lived on what salt rations it had on hand.[6]

What Graves could do, he did. On 30 April 1775, Gage asked for the services of an "advice boat" for communication with New York; by 9 May Graves had a "swift sailing sloop" procured, equipped, manned, and ready. His warships helped to supply Gage's troops by seizing American vessels loaded with foodstuffs, and by raiding nearby islands for hay and livestock.[7] Other warships retrieved cannon and ammunition from the almost unguarded coastal forts (such as William and Mary Castle off Portsmouth, and Fort Pownall on the Penobscot) to keep them out of American hands.[8] When Gage requested Graves' aid in defending Boston against an American amphibious attack ".. from the Charles Town side ...," the Admiral took the risk of anchoring one of his largest ships, the 64-gun *Somerset* ".. exactly in the Ferry way between the two towns."[9] The "Select Men" of Charlestown were warned that the *Somerset* would fire on their town ".. if they suffered the Rebels to take possession of [it] or erect any works upon the Heights." On 23 April, after getting permission from Gage, he put marine fatigue details to work constructing a battery on Copp's Hill in north Boston which was ".. of equal height with Bunkershill and the highest land on the Charlestown side." Here he emplaced several 24-pounder guns (apparently taken from his ships) to support the *Somerset*. Officers of the Boston garrison seem to have been amused by "the Admiral's battery," but it was shrewdly placed, and Gage eventually took it over.[10] Before long, the *Somerset*'s position in the ferry-way proved impractical: She could not be shifted ".. except upon a flood tide and then only by warping, and ... some hours before and after low water her guns could not command the heights [Breed's Hill] over Charlestown ..." On 2 June Graves replaced her with the 20-gun *Lively*.[11]

Both Graves and Gage worried over continual reports that the Americans were collecting whale boats and other light craft in the rivers and inlets around Boston harbor, and that Americans in canoes had been reconnoitering Castle William at night. Both officers feared a large-scale amphibious attack on the Castle, the undermanned warships in the harbor, or even against Boston itself from across the shallows of the "back Bay," where only light vessels could operate. Graves was equally concerned over the chance of a few "fanatics" sabotaging some of his anchored ships.[12]

By way of precaution, all the local American boats and vessels—fishing boats, which could operate under permit to help feed hungry Boston, excepted—were collected and kept under guard ".. southward of the long warf." From ".. Gunfiring in the evening ... till day light ..." only the patrolling Navy guard boats were permitted to move in the harbor and the number of these boats was doubled. A flat-bottomed boat was used to scout as far as possible up the Charles River. Ships anchored in exposed positions rigged their boarding nettings.[13]

Guard-boat service was hard on Graves' understrength crews, and its results never were very satisfactory. The Americans knew Boston harbor's secrets; the British did not. As Graves observed in his reports "The sharp construction and great draught [draft] of water of the men of wars boats rendered them very unfit for going up the narrow Creeks which abound in the neighborhood of Boston, where if they [ran aground] and there was not room for them to turn about, it would be hardly practicable to retreat, and the crew be in danger of becoming prey to the enemy." By contrast, the American whale boats "From their lightness and drawing little Water, they can not only outrow our Boats, but by getting into Shoal Water, and in Calms, they must constantly escape."[14] Eventually, he invented a double-ender, shallow-draft barge for harbor operations, and took American boats into use; but this was after the battle of Bunker's Hill.

Boston might be Graves' major responsibility, but other problems nagged him increasingly. His only naval base was Halifax, Nova Scotia, some 500 miles of North Atlantic waters to the northeast—an excellent harbor, but poorly located to support operations along the southeastern and southern American coasts.

Elsewhere, it was extremely hard to get repairs done, or even to procure the necessary materials and skilled labor—especially after Lexington/Concord. To compound the problem, Halifax itself was in considerable danger from a strong pro-American element which was active throughout Nova Scotia. A large supply of hay, collected for shipment to Boston, was burned; there were indications that the naval base might be next. Gage having transferred most of the Halifax garrison to Boston, Graves felt obliged to station one of his better ships, the 28-gun light frigate *Tartar*, there to guard it.[15]

Meanwhile, cries for help came from royal officials in every colony as British rule broke down. Governor John Wentworth of New Hampshire considered the 20-gun *Scarborough* and the 8-gun *Canceaux* insufficient to cow Portsmouth, and so demanded another sloop of war and 50 marines: Graves could not oblige. Governor Cadwallader Colden of New York wanted a ".. large Man of War ... which can on occasion put two or three hundred men ashore ..." to control the Hudson River. Graves finally sent him the 64-gun *Asia,* which soon became the refuge of such of the New York garrison (five companies of the 18th Foot) as had not deserted. The Port Collector at Savannah, Georgia, asked the 6-gun schooner *St. John* for sailors to guard seized merchandise: A mob beat up the guards and threw them into the sea. One drowned.

In mid-May angry New Englanders recaptured a vessel taken into custody by the *Falcon*, making prisoners of the British prize crew. The sheriff at Falmouth (now Maine, then Massachusetts) asked Gage for a warship to protect the completion of a local vessel, owned by a loyal citizen. Gage referred the matter to Graves, who sent off a hired schooner ".. manned, armed, and victualled ..." from the *Preston* at Boston, with orders for the *Canceaux* to handle this errand before proceeding to Halifax for overdue repairs. The small schooner *Margueritta*, escorting some lumber vessels, was overwhelmed by two American ships in the Machias River, and the midshipman commanding her killed, on 11 June. Captain James Wallace of the 20-gun *Rose* off Providence, Rhode Island, reported the situation getting out of hand: He himself was threatened with a coat of tar and feathers when he went ashore, and was warned of a plot to seize his ship by surprise boarding. Providence seamen had burned the royal revenue cutter *Gaspee* in 1772, so Wallace took the warning seriously. He would do his best, but there were ".. three large and distinct channels ..." to Providence, and the *Rose* could not watch all of them. He secured a small vessel to use as a tender, but on 15 June it was forced ashore and captured by two American ships, though her crew escaped. (On 13 June, Rhode Island had commissioned the armed sloop *Katy*, under Captain Abraham Whipple, ".. to protect the Province's trade ... in his Majesty's name George the Third King of Great Britain and So forth.")

In Virginia, bumbling Governor Dunmore, who had found it safer to take refuge aboard the schooner *Magdalen*, was demanding a "large ship of war." Graves considered sending him the 70-gun *Boyne*, but decided the 16-gun *Otter* must suffice. Dunmore then made a typical contribution to the confusion: Without informing Graves, he persuaded the captain of the *Magdalen* to sail for England with "highly urgent reports," incidently taking Dunmore's wife, family, and valuables along. As a minor irritant, Americans had begun sniping at British ships, usually at such extreme range that no harm was done. Lacking definite instructions, Graves authorized returning such fire only in case of absolute self-defense. His captains seem to have interpreted this term liberally, especially after the *Scarborough* had a man wounded off Piscataqua.[16]

To discharge all these missions, Graves had a makeshift squadron, ill-found and under-manned. On 1 January 1775 it totalled 24 vessels, distributed from Halifax to East Florida. Its most powerful units were the 70-gun *Asia*, the 64-gun *Somerset* and *Boyne*, the 50-gun *Preston*, and the 28-gun *Tartar*. Next came the 20-gun sloops-of-war *Mercury*, *Glasgow*, *Rose*, *Fowey*, *Lively*, and *Scarborough*; the 16-gun sloops *Swan*, *Kingfisher*, and *Tamer*; and 8-gun *Canceaux*, *Savage*, and *Cruizer*. Last and least were a gaggle of 6-gun sloops, brigs, and schooners—the *Diana*, *Hope*, *Magdalan*, *St. John*, *Gaspee*, *Halifax*, and *Diligent*. Of these—as noted—Dunmore disposed of the *Magdalan;* the *Halifax*—".. a very bad low vessel—unfit for service" was wrecked near Machais on 15 February; the *Diana* (see chapter VI) was lost in action in May.[17]

Many of these ships were in poor condition. The *Somerset*, *Boyne*, and *Asia* had been on service as guard ships off England; as the first vessels available, they had been dispatched hurriedly, without preliminary refitting. All were leaky, especially the *Somerset*. Graves had the latter unloaded, with the help of some borrowed Army transports, and heeled over in early April "to calk as much of her bottom as possible," but the *Somerset* continued to leak. The *Hope* and *Cruizer* were in very bad condition, the latter's captain being afraid to fire his larger guns because of the probable damage to his ship. The *Canceaux* struck a rock off New York, but had to continue serving for two months in her crippled condition. The *Fowey* needed repairs and stores, but could not leave her station off Virginia. There was a general shortage of supplies throughout the squadron. On 23 May, Graves had to ask for some of the Army's reserve of slow match in Castle William—the squadron was almost out of it and there was none at Halifax.[18]

The biggest ships, designed for line-of-battle operations on the high seas, proved too unhandy for operations in Boston harbor, where they could not work close enough inshore for their heavy guns to be effective, or for ordinary coastal patrol. Most of the hard work therefore fell on the 16 and 20-gun sloops. The smaller vessels, with their few light guns and 30-man crews—though suitable enough for anti-smuggling duty in peace time—were too weak for lone combat operations in close waters, the Americans having plenty of fast, handy armed vessels of equal or superior size. Graves requested a few of the "old Fifty Gun Ships" which he thought would be excellent for service on the ".. Rivers of this Continent; they are handy Ships, and from their easy Draught of Water can go in and out of Harbours without that great Risque and Delay which constantly attends the piloting of those now with me." He also wanted additional ships' boats ".. as the principal part of the Duty here is done by Boats": All warships coming from England should have an extra boat, and additional ones should be sent out for his squadron. (As an example of the delays of 18th century trans-Atlantic warfare, Graves wrote on 18 May 1775; his answer was dated 6 July.)

Gage seconded Graves' requests. ".. It will be Necessary also to augment the Squadron with a Number of Frigates, for we hear that they are fitting out Vessels of Force, in Various Places, much superior to the Armed Sloops and Schooners; and I will add the great Service that may be made of flatbottomed Boats, used last War in landing Troops, big enough to hold Sixty Men, including the Rowers, of which we are at this Moment in very great Need."[19]

Graves' crews supposedly were at "peace establishment" strength, which meant they would be too weak for prolonged military operations. In fact, most of his ships had left England with crews considerably below that minimum standard. Since then they

had been under steady attrition by sickness, desertion, and death. In April, Graves reported his squadron over 160 men short; in May, his marines were some 60 men understrength. Desertion was a constant problem—always endemic in the Royal Navy, it now undoubtedly was stimulated by the constant hardships resulting from combat service with reduced crews. Some ships were seriously weakened: On 22 May two marines and the purser's steward deserted from the *Falcon*. Sickness—mostly a "feverish scurvy"—developed in the ships at Boston by late February, and the difficulty of procuring fresh food made its treatment slow. On 16 June there were 41 seamen, from twelve ships, in the Boston naval hospital.[20] There was no immediate hope of getting replacements from England, and few—if any—could be recruited voluntarily in America. Graves therefore authorized various captains to "press" sailors. Such action being likely to stir up further unwanted trouble, this was to be done ".. with all possible moderation." The *Scarborough* solved the problem by taking a few men off each ship coming in from the West Indies.[21]

In England, the corrupt and languid Admiralty began bestirring itself. Graves was given authority to buy three schooners for inshore work.[22] A series of sloops (possibly because they were the easiest to outfit and man) were dispatched to America, followed by a storeship. As they arrived, they immediately were put to work. The *Falcon* and *Nautilus* reached Boston in mid-April, ".. shorthanded and very leaky ..." from a rough passage, followed by the *Otter,* the *Merlin,* and the *Senegal*. Others were on the way.[22] After cruising "..from Cape Ann to Cape Cod ..." to meet and escort a transport with clothing and ordnance stores which Gage feared the Americans might intercept, the *Senegal* was dispatched to Falmouth. The *Otter* went to reinforce Dunmore's attempt to maintain a toehold in Virginia, the *Nautilus* to block the Delaware River through which the Americans were conducting a furious trade in military supplies. The *Merlin* was dispatched to overawe the troublesome port of Marblehead, the *Falcon* (after a sheep-lifting sortie among the coastal islands to help feed Boston) to the Penobscot.

By mid-June Graves commanded 29 ships, three of them at Halifax for repairs or fitting out (plus the *Tartar*, still there as a guard ship). Overall, there was little improvement: As Governor Josiah Martin of North Carolina noted, the rattletrap little *Cruizer* still had to watch a coast of "near three Hundred Miles in Extent and full of little Inletts," which normally would require four or five larger ships.[23] On 16 June Graves had only six ships in Boston harbor, including the relatively useless *Somerset*, *Boyne*, and *Preston* which he had half-stripped of their crews to man his smaller vessels and various Army craft.[24] (See Appendix II)

These Army craft, under Gage's command, were an odd little navy in themselves. There were an unreported number of transports, mostly small and fairly handy, used for a variety of errands and functions—floating magazines and isolation hospitals, general harbor work, voyages to Nova Scotia to secure forage, wood, and coal.[25] The most important of these was the shallow-draft *Symmetry*, armed with eighteen 9-pounders. (English practice was to use such "hired ships" for convoy duty when warships were not available.) It is doubtful that the *Symmetry's* discipline and gunnery were up to Royal Navy standards; available information indicates that she was something of a problem ship. Shortly after Bunker's Hill, Gage declared her "unserviceable," but Graves suggested that assigning a Navy lieutenant to command her might straighten out the situation.[26] Most of those transports were shorthanded, so that Gage occasionally had to ask Graves for help in manning them. An example was the *Pallas* on 11 June: Gage

(1) Boston. (2) Noddle's Island. (3) Castle William. (4) Dorchester Peninsula. (5) Bunker's Hill on Charlestown Peninsula, misidentified as Breed's Hill. (6) Breed's Hill, misidentified as Bunker's Hill. (7) Moulton's Hill. (8) Charles Bay or Back Bay. (9) Charles River. (10) Mystic River. (11) Cambridge. (12) Roxbury. (13) Road to Medford. (14) Forts #1 & #2. (15) Fort #3. (16) Hog Island. (17) Winnisimet. (18) Deer Island. (19) Lechmere's Point. (20) Chelsea. (21) Prospect Hill. (22) Winter Hill. This is a section of a map titled *A Plan of the Bay and Harbor of Boston Surveyed agreeably to the Orders and Instructions of the Right Honorable the Lords Commissioners for Trade and Plantations To Samuel Holland, Esqr. His Majesty's Surveyor General of Lands for the Northern District of North America. By Messrs. Wheeler and Grant, Deputy Surveyors of Said District.* Although undated, the map is believed to have been made in 1775 about the

time of the outbreak of hostilities at Lexington/Concord. The map carries the notation "The Want of Naval Assistance in the Survey . . . is the Reason in being Deficient in soundings, shoals, & c . . ." After Lexington/Concord, the work was set aside, thus depriving the British of much needed information relative to soundings in the Mystic River during the Battle of Bunker's Hill, a few weeks later. The map is in pen-and-ink and water color. Thus, in reproduction, the shoal areas appear gray, and the areas become darker as elevations rise. The transposition of Bunker's and Breed's Hills by Thomas Wheeler and James Grant is an error that was copied by other British map makers. Circled numbers are additions to the map. Map published through the courtesy of Geography and Map Division, Library of Congress. (G3764.B6P55 1775 .W5 Vault; *British Maps of the American Revolution* 116/4.)

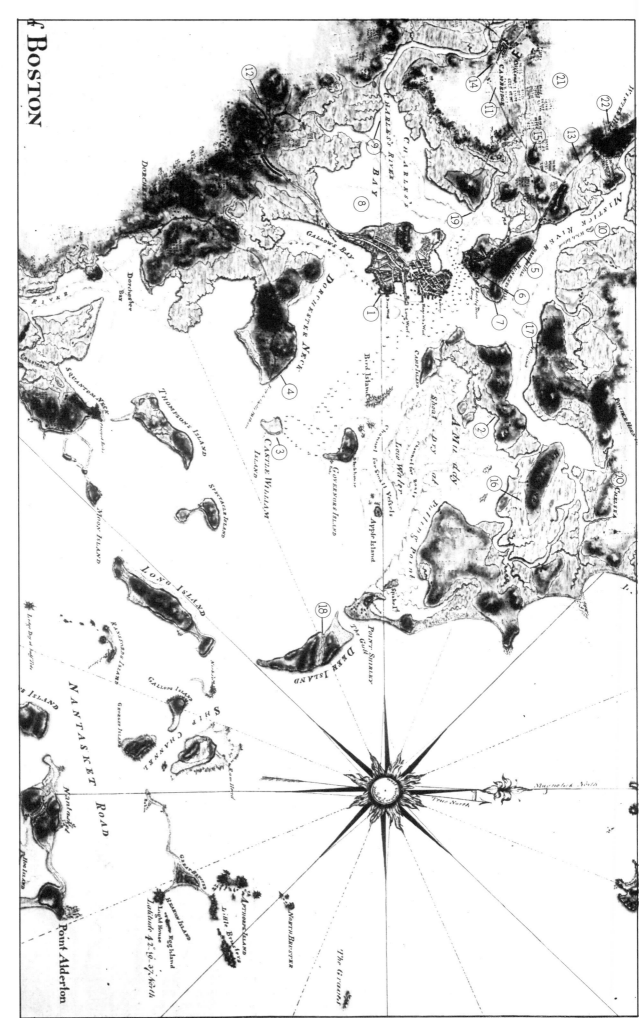

coupled his request with a scolding that Graves was impressing sailors from the transports to fill up his warships' crews.[27] Graves got *Pallas* manned and returned a soft answer: He did not press transport crew members, but some of them did enlist voluntarily; though pay in the transport service was higher, its discipline was far more captious and brutal and its living conditions worse than the Navy's.[28]

Another problem was the Army's "gondolas," which Graves usually termed "scows." Their exact number is uncertain. Apparently two were engaged at Bunker's Hill, and a third put into service a day or two thereafter. These were improvised gunboats—large flatboats, the sides of which had been built up with planks thick enough to stop musket balls. They mounted one or two guns and could operate in shallow water, but were slow and clumsy. Details of seamen handled them, yet they were commanded by an officer of the Royal Artillery, and their guns may have been manned by soldiers. Major General William Howe complained of their poor service during the battle of Bunker's Hill, and Gage requested that Graves give them "such repair as to make them serviceable"—also larger crews and a long list of equipment. Graves seems to have felt it necessary to remind Gage that the gondolas ". . were fitted ashore by the Engineer's Carpenters" who obviously had made a landlubber's job of them. He would furnish the additional sailors for them, and also the needed ". . Grape Shot, Guntackles, Hand Spikes, Musquets, and Cutlasses . . . on receiving proper receipts . . ." (Here Graves inserted a quick note that the Army hadn't signed for naval supplies previously issued, to the confusion of his accounts.) Gage also wanted "canister shot," which Graves did not have; oars, which Graves said could be purchased in Boston; and tanned leather curtains, to screen the gondolas' powder magazines. The last appeared unobtainable, but Graves promised that—if Gage could not find suitable leather in Boston—". . One of the Ships shall part with hers."[29]

Riding at anchor in Boston harbor as the night of 16 June closed down, Graves' six warships were symbols of England's military might. Yet their effectiveness in the next day's action would depend on such unpredictable factors as the direction and volume of the prevailing wind.

CHAPTER IV

THE EMBATTLED FARMERS

Artemas Ward, general and commander in chief of the Massachusetts forces, was perfectly aware that one misjudgement on his part could abort the American Revolution. Though active in the Massachusetts militia from boyhood, his only previous war service had been as major of a Massachusetts provincial regiment during Abercromby's mangled 1758 campaign against Ticonderoga. Though he had been careful that his men were properly equipped and that the regimental surgeons, armorers, and chaplains were qualified and actually present, he saw little fighting and much unnecessary suffering from ignorance of camp sanitation and field cooking. He came home a lieutenant colonel but never again was really in good health. Now, at forty-eight, he was a sharp-faced man of medium height, too stout for his age, and subject to days of agony from "the stone." Careful, slow-moving, slow to decide, he was utterly without the showier qualities of leadership. Yet he was trusted because he was an epitome of New England's solid virtues: Of good family, a graduate of Harvard, he had worked his way as school teacher, storekeeper, tax assessor, justice of the peace, selectman,

town clerk, provincial legislator, militia officer, town and church moderator, judge of the Court of Common Pleas, provincial councilor. In each step he had proved honest, industrious, and efficient. He had been a leader of the Patriot movement from its beginnings, and had helped to purge the Massachusetts militia of its Loyalist officers, thereby breaking the Royal Governor's means of using it. In October 1754 he became the second-in-command of the Massachusetts militia. (Its commander, General Jedediah Preble of Falmouth—now in Maine, then part of Massachusetts—was too old and infirm for active duty.) Ward was sick when news reached him on 19 April of the Lexington/Concord fight, but the next morning he rode to Cambridge to take command of the New England militia converging on Boston.[1]

These forces came flooding in, and almost immediately began ebbing homewards. They had turned out to meet an urgent emergency, leaving their plows literally in the furrow. The British had been driven back into Boston and apparently were in no great hurry to venture out again: They themselves were tired, hungry, and thirsty, and there were unfinished chores to do at home. Ward's first responsibility therefore was to hold enough of this army of militiamen around Boston to keep Gage penned while an army of volunteers was organized to replace them. As part of this, he would have to see that both armies were somehow fed and sheltered. Fortunately, Ward thoroughly understood his fellow New Englanders. He might be accused of undue deference to political opinion, or laxness in enforcing discipline, but he always somehow exerted the necessary minimum of quiet authority. On 24 April, amid a minor chaos of arriving and departing companies, detachments, and individuals, he bluntly wrote the Massachusetts Provincial Congress, "My situation is such, that if I had not enlisting orders immediately, I shall be left all alone. It is impossible to keep the men here, excepting something be done. I therefore pray that the plan be completed and handed to me this morning. . ."[2]

The Massachusetts Provincial Congress managed the colony's war effort through its Committee of Safety, which held executive authority from it on military matters. Ward was directly responsible to the Committee of Safety, though on important matters he might address himself to the Provincial Congress. For mutual convenience, the Committee of Safety established itself at Cambridge, near Ward's headquarters. Ward normally discussed proposed operations with his Council of War, an advisory group composed of the senior officers of the different New England contingents. Parallel to the Committee of Safety was the Committee of Supplies, responsible for rations, weapons, and equipment. John Pigeon, its Commissary General, was a man of quiet ability, now mostly forgotten.

All of these men and agencies had ". . too much business upon their hands . . . The Committee of Safety who are the premium mobile in the military movements are crowded with business . . ."[3] But the Provincial Congress, the actual source of all authority, was under the cross-haul of many competing problems. The seacoast towns were crying for troops, artillery, and ammunition to protect them from the blockade and foraging of British warships. Loyalists had to be detected and controlled. (Ironically, Dr. Benjamin Church, one of the Committee of Safety's most fervent members, also reported its decisions to General Gage.)[4] More important, the stability and supremacy of civil government must be maintained. Thousands of undisciplined armed men were on the move throughout the state; some of them were disorderly, and there was occasional plundering.[5] Naturally, wild rumors were loose—one of them that Gage planned to ". . Send ye Smallpox

Into ye Army."[6] (Possibly some Americans remembered that, during Pontiac's Rebellion in 1763-1764, General Jeffrey Amherst had urged that ". . it be contrived to send the *Small Pox* among those disaffected tribes of Indians . . .")[7] Amid all this, the Provincial Congress organized its volunteer army, a task which it had been considering since 14 April. Its strength was set first at 8,000, but soon raised to 13,600.[8]

Massachusetts already had what amounted to two militia armies on its hands. In preparation for possible hostilities, the Colony had ordered that a third of its militiamen be designated for immediate service in emergencies, and had organized these "minute men" into separate companies and regiments. Both minute men and ordinary militia had turned out for Lexington/Concord, and elements of both still were with Ward. The Provincial Congress hoped to persuade them to volunteer for eight months' additional service. Initially, the Committee of Safety recommended regiments with nine companies, each of 79 officers and men. This, however, met several objections: The average minute man/militia company was somewhat smaller; formation of larger companies would require the consolidation of these existing units, and would make some of their officers surplus. Local spirit was strong in New England, and neither officers nor enlisted men wished to serve with strangers. Officers did not propose to accept dismissal or demotion—militia rank was a highly important matter in local social standing and political preference. Therefore the Congress adopted a 10-company regiment, with 3 officers and 56 enlisted men to a company. There was a nose-count of the men around Boston willing to enlist, and quotas of the additional recruits required were computed for each town. "Gentlemen" (mostly former commanders of minute men regiments) were designated as colonels in the new army and given "sets of orders" for their captains who were to do the actual recruiting. All officers' commissions were to be temporary until their respective regiments were recruited to full strength. In keeping with the awkward old British custom, general officers also were to command regiments, being allowed an extra major to make it easier.[9] The Provincial Congress then turned to its other difficulties.

The raising of this new army oscilated between high patriotism and low comedy. Colonel Jonathan Brewer, once a captain in Rogers' Rangers, proposed to raise a regiment of rangers and lead them against Quebec, instead of Boston. He also took "into his service" two horses without their owners' permission, involved himself in a peculiar real estate transaction, and came near losing his regiment. Colonel John Patterson created a minor fuss by picking up two companies raised in New York and Connecticut. Two different officers claimed the lieutenant colonelcy of General Ward's regiment: Ward declined choosing between them, and the matter had to be referred to the Provincial Congress. There were disputes concerning which colonel had authority to recruit in the isolated northern counties which are now the state of Maine. Colonel Samuel Gerrish became displeasing to his subordinates and six of his captains seceded, choosing Captain Moses Little as their colonel. This command dispute was not resolved until 15 June, when the Committee of Safety accepted Little's claim, finding that ". . the said Little has raised eight companies . . . amounting inclusive of officers to the number of 509 men . . . armed with good effective firelocks, and 382 of them with good bayonets, fitted to their firelocks . . ." Gerrish managed to muster a weak regiment nevertheless, but was not to retain it long. A similar revolt took place in John Nixon's Regiment. Objecting to its lieutenant colonel, four companies departed—one to Ephraim Doolittle's Regiment, two to Jonathan Brewer's, and one to Thomas Gardner's. The last returned to Nixon when a majority of its privates organized a counter-protest.

These examples may have inspired Lieutenant Colonel Lemuel Robinson of General William Heath's militia regiment. The details are murky, but apparently Heath left the raising of his volunteer regiment to Robinson, and Robinson decided to set up as colonel on his own right. He pieced together a regiment, including four independent companies the Provincial Congress had authorized for coast defense, and an independent company of Connecticut rangers that had been waiting around since Lexington/Concord. The matter came to a head on 16 June when the Provincial Congress discovered "General Heath and Colonel Robinson returned a list of their companies, and . . . there are several of the same companies returned in each." The resulting explosion blew Robinson out of the army. Colonel Ebenezer Learned's sin was of a gentler sort—he merely proposed to raise a "regiment of grenadiers." The Provincial Congress did not consider the term fitting, and the matter was allowed to subside.[10]

At best, recruiting went slowly after the first rush of enlistments in late April. With no regiments "certified," there was doubt and uncertainty and trouble over rank and pay. To spur things along, the Committee of Safety offered on 29 April that any captain who brought in a full company could start drawing pay immediately, even if its parent regiment were not complete.[11] On 16 May, however, it had to confess that it had no definite information on the army's status. Three days later—less than a month before Bunker's Hill—Ward finally read the Provincial Congress a stiff lesson. "It appears to me absolutely necessary that the regiments be immediately settled; the officers commissioned; the soldiers numbered and paid, agreeable to what has been proposed by the Congress . . . if we would save our country . . ."[12]

Thereafter things went more rapidly. Two regiments were certified that same day. On the 20th, Ward received his formal commission as general and commander in chief of the Massachusetts forces; John Thomas was confirmed as lieutenant general on the 25th. On 10 June, the Committee of Safety made its first complete report—twenty regiments officially in the process of formation, eight more seeking approval, but a good deal of confusion. On the 15th the situation had cleared up considerably; some twenty-four infantry regiments were reported more-or-less ready for service. These, the Committee felt, should be accepted and their officers be "commissionated" as soon as possible, even though the Provincial Congress had just set the army's strength at twenty-three regiments of infantry and one of artillery.[13] Colonel John Glover's regiment was to be left at Marblehead for the time being to protect the coast and complete its armament. On 9 June, Ward's Massachusetts troops reportedly mustered a total of 11,636 with more en route to join. (See Appendix III) Recruits included a thin sprinkling of British deserters and free Negroes, some of the former proving handy as drillmasters. There also was a company of Stockbridge Indians (now almost as settled as their White neighbors) in Patterson's regiment—though they would fight only ". . in our own way." They seem to have come and gone irregularly; because of their weakness for drinking themselves blind every payday, they asked that their pay be doled out to them through two trusted white neighbors. One of the British deserters—Martin Hurly, a grenadier private of the 44th Foot—rose to the grade of lieutenant in the American service. In 1777 he was captured at Germantown, and promptly hanged.[14]

To lead this volunteer army, under Ward and Thomas, the Provincial Congress chose, on 13-14 June, Colonel John Whitcomb and Dr. Joseph Warren as "first" and "second" major generals. In addition, there were two militia generals—Seth Pomeroy and William Heath—who had been appointed in 1774.

Thomas had begun his military career as a surgeon during the French and Indian War, but later served for three campaigns as a regimental commander. His letters show a cool, independent personality, not overly bothered by niceties of literacy. Most of his contemporaries thought highly of his abilities, but he died of smallpox in Canada in 1776 while attempting to check the British counteroffensive. Whitcomb remains a dim figure; he already had requested his "discharge" in early June, and did nothing particularly useful during the rest of his service. Warren, by contrast, was only thirty-four, but chairman of the Committee of Safety and an acknowledged leader of the Massachusetts revolt. Gifted with intelligence, courage, sincerity, and winning nature, he was widely popular: Though he had no military experience, his personal qualities might have made him an effective commander had he not been killed in action at Bunker's Hill. Pomeroy began as a blacksmith and gunsmith. He served at the capture of Louisbourg in 1745, and on the frontier during 1746-1748. During the French and Indian War he fought his way up to the grade of colonel, and was thereafter a popular figure in the Massachusetts militia, being named its third-in-command in 1774. Now, he was sixty-eight; he would fight, but his health was failing. After Bunker's Hill he would not accept a Continental commission as the senior brigadier general—but he died on active duty at Peekskill, New York, in 1777, commanding militia called out to guard the Hudson. Heath had seen no active service, but had been active in both politics and militia affairs and had served on the Committee of Safety. He was a sincere patriot, and he did his best—without much success—to be a good general. When he wrote his memoirs he followed Julius Caesar's example and referred approvingly to himself as "Our General."[15]

Generals, unfortunately, were easier to make than artillerymen and cannon. From the beginning of 1775 the Provincial Congress had searched for qualified officers; on 13 April it authorized a regiment of six companies, which it increased to ten on 10 May. Even so, there was so much trouble finding suitable recruits that the artillery was authorized to enlist men out of the infantry regiments, not to exceed four men per company. There was a serious shortage of equipment, and the available field guns were mostly light 2, 3, and 4-pounders. When called into action on 16-17 June, half of the companies apparently still were understrength; the regiment had not been officially certified, and the officers had not received their commissions. Richard Gridley was appointed colonel of the artillery regiment, and also served as the army's chief engineer. He drove a strict bargain in accepting, requiring that he be paid 170 pounds a year while on active duty and 123 pounds a year for the rest of his life thereafter, to compensate him for having to give up the British "half pay" granted him for his services at Louisbourg in 1745. Gridley was largely self-taught; though he probably was the most skilled gunner and engineer available in Massachusetts, his actual competence was little more than a jack-leg smattering of the required professional knowledge. Also, he was a believer in keeping good things in his own family—one son, Scarborough Gridley, was the regiment's "second major," another, Samuel Gridley, commanded one of its companies.[16]

New Hampshire's Army was, in fact, a Massachusetts creation. Militia from New Hampshire had come down against Boston following Lexington/Concord, somewhat disappointed to have missed the fighting. Rather than see them all go home, the Committee of Safety—as it wrote the New Hampshire Provincial Congress on 24 April—". . thought it best to give orders . . . for enlisting those of them who were willing . . . until the resolve of your Congress is known, when we are ready and desirous they should be discharged from us and put under such command as you shall direct . . ."[17]

The result was a strong 13-company regiment under Colonel John Stark, a small one under Colonel James Reed, and a bobtailed unit of four companies under Colonel Paul D. Sargent—totaling roughly 1400 officers and men.[18] These units took their orders directly from Ward. New Hampshire's official reaction was slow; its Provincial Congress did not consider any effective measures until 18-31 May, when it threshed out a decision to raise 2000 men in three regiments of ten companies each ". . Including Officers & those of this Province already in the service," and designated Brigadier General Nathaniel Folsom to command them.[19] During the next three days they regularized Stark's and Reed's units as, respectively, the 1st and 3d New Hampshire regiments, confirming their officers and taking steps to bring Reed's up to full strength.[20]

New Hampshire seems to have had more than the usual difficulties in providing clothing, weapons, and equipment. No qualified artillerymen could be found. Its 2d Regiment, organized under Colonel Enoch Poor, did not march to join Ward until news came of Bunker's Hill. General Folsom reached Cambridge on 20 June, and at once found John Stark much more troublesome than the British.[21]

For all this, the New Hampshire contingent probably was the best fighting material in Ward's command. Thinly settled New Hampshire still was something of a frontier; New Hampshire men had been the backbone of Rogers' Rangers during the French and Indian War, and there were proved combat veterans in the regiments before Boston. In John Stark they had a leader of skill and daring—a long, lean fighting man who had been a ranger captain under Rogers, and combined New England cantankerousness with Scots-Irish contentiousness.[22]

Connecticut was more methodical. On 26 April its General Assembly ordered that ". . one fourth part of the militia of this Colony be . . . inlisted, equipped, accoutred and assembled . . . distributed into companies consisting of one hundred men each. That said companys shall be formed into six regiments, to be commanded by one major-general, assisted by two brigadier-generals, each of which shall take command of a regiment as a colonel . . ."[23] Officers were commissioned immediately, and recruiting completed.

The British army in Boston was not Connecticut's sole concern. At New York's request, Connecticut troops were dispatched to garrison Ticonderoga and Crown Point; the Continental Congress directed that others be sent to aid in securing New York City and Hudson River.[24] Only two regiments went to Boston—the 2nd Regiment of Brigadier General Joseph Spencer and the 3d Regiment of "Second Brigadier General" Israel Putnam. Two companies of the 6th Regiment followed on 7 June. These troops were practically an allied force; Connecticut did not formally put them under Ward's command until 17 June.[25] One company of Putnam's regiment—that of Captain John Chester from Wethersfield—was most conspicuous in its "uniform wholly blue, turned up with red."[26] Apparently it was the only uniformed infantry unit in the entire army before Boston.

Though Spencer was the senior Connecticut officer, Israel Putnam was the dominant personality. A stocky, round-faced farmer, enthusiastic and tireless, he had served with Connecticut provincial troops throughout the French and Indian War, winning fame as the commander of a "spy company" or "Connecticut Rangers."[27] During this service he picked up useful bits of military lore: In 1758 a private recorded that Major Putnam taught the new-raised Connecticut regiments how to form their "front to the right and left" for an inspection by General Abercromby.[28] He showed no particular skill, but great courage. More, he was a cheerful, friendly person, with a talent for amazing yarns, practical jokes, and two-handed drinking. He made stout friends among the British officers. Some of them were now in Boston.

Rhode Island had been equally businesslike. On 22 April its General Assembly voted to raise 1500 men; on 3 May it ordered these organized into a brigade of three regiments, each of eight companies. One company was to be a "train of artillery, and have the use of the colony's field pieces." The regiments were to have perfect equality in rank and assignment, and therefore do not seem to have been numbered. Men were enlisted ". . in His Majesty's service . . . for the preservation of the liberties of America . . ." The artillery company was organized from and around a militia unit, the "United Train of Artillery;" besides its four brass 4-pounder field pieces, it brought along twelve heavy guns—old iron 18-and-24-pounders, of dubious quality but the only siege guns then available to Ward's army.

As the brigadier general to command this force, termed "the army of observation," the Rhode Island Assembly picked "Nathanael Greene, Jr., Esq." then a private in the Kentish Guards, a volunteer militia company.[29] Only 32 years old, self-educated, sensitive, slightly lame, a Quaker cast out by his church for taking up arms against his lawful king, Greene was both studious and practical. By the war's end, he would be acclaimed Washington's ablest lieutenant.

The Rhode Island units were sent off to Boston as they were organized. Ward stationed them on his right flank around Roxbury, but there soon were difficulties. Greene arrived (apparently on 23 May) to find their camp ". . in great commotion . . . The want of government, and of a certainty of supplies had thrown every thing into disorder. Several Companies had clubbed their muskets in order to march home. I have made several regulations for introducing order and composing their murmurs; but it is very difficult to limit people who have had so much latitude . . . The Commissaries had been beaten off at my arrival, and were about returning home the next day. I believe there never was a person more welcome, who was so little deserving, as myself . . ."[30] By June Greene had some 1390 effective troops at Roxbury.[31] They were better equipped than the other colonial contingents, having ". . proper tents and marquees . . . and everything in ye most exact English taste."[32] Also, they were admittedly the best trained and disciplined. Like Connecticut, Rhode Island retained control of its own army until after Bunker's Hill, though Greene was always cooperative.

No one, not even Ward, had more than a general idea of the strength of his combined armies. Throughout April and May volunteer and militia units came and went, with incomplete records or none at all, ". . the order, regularity, and discipline of the troops from [Massachusetts] is so deficient that no return can be made which is to be relied upon."[33] (After Washington assumed command of this army, it took him eight days of unrelenting effort to get a fairly accurate count of its numbers.) To further confuse the issue, some minute men and militia—both individuals and units—still lingered around Cambridge, reluctant either to enlist or go home despite repeated appeals and orders.[34]

Almost every regiment included a number of unarmed men (See Appendix III). Though the militia laws required each citizen to have a musket and proper equipment, many of the volunteers thriftily left theirs safe at home, depending on Massachusetts to arm and equip them. Good cartridge boxes, essential to protect the soldiers' cartridges from wear and weather, were in especially short supply. Powder horns and shot pouches made fairly acceptable substitutes, but some men had only small tin boxes for their ammunition, or carried it loose in their pockets. Such factors, combined with the variety of musket calibers, made ammunition supply

a constant trouble. There was an equal shortage of tents, blankets, and camp equipment. Commissary General Pigeon managed to keep the men well fed, but everything else came slowly, and the Committee of Supply was once moved to complain to the Provincial Congress that Ward was "ungenerous" in urging them to greater speed.[35]

The New England volunteer of this period usually is presented as a dead shot. This, he was not. Men from New Hampshire might still find good hunting, but any trace of the frontier and plentiful game were long gone from most of Massachusetts, Connecticut, and Rhode Island. Militia training did not stress marksmanship, and Ward had no powder to spare for musketry training of any sort. At best the average New Englander was fairly familiar with firearms—he could load and fire a musket with a fair chance of hitting an easy target at short range.[36] But this made him probably as good a shot as the average French or Prussian veteran.

One particular shortage which would have increasing importance was the lack of medical officers and supplies. Also, the average soldier—and especially the officers—needed knowledge of how to care for themselves in the field. (Ward did not think to order latrines dug until 2 May.) As the Massachusetts Provincial Congress was later to caution Washington when he arrived to take command, "The greatest part of them have not before seen service; and though naturally brave and of good understanding, yet, for want of experience in military life have but little knowledge of divers things most essential to the preservation of health, and even life. The youth of America are not possessed of the absolute necessity of cleanliness in their dress and lodging, continual exercise and strict temperance to preserve them from diseases frequently prevailing in camps."[37]

It was an improvised army of free New Englanders ". . . apter to argue than obey." It had no trained staff, artillerymen, or engineers. Its regiments were hasty collections of companies, some not yet fully organized. It included a good many veteran officers, but none had commanded more than a regiment in action, and comparatively few had seen much actual combat. It particularly lacked a cadre of experienced non-commissioned officers. Drill, discipline, and good leadership could give it cohesion and regimental pride—but there would not be time enough for drill and discipline, and the leadership was untested.

CHAPTER V
THE KING'S BAD BARGAINS

The British Army in Boston was an emergency clubbing together of understrength regiments, which differed amazingly in their systems of drill, their discipline, and their efficiency. (The British Army did not have a standard infantry drill regulation until 1792.) Officers and men had spent an uncomfortable winter and spring, increasingly at odds with both Bostonians and their own commander. They might not appreciate the complexities of Gage's position, but they quickly comprehended that his policy of appeasement would fail. The fact that Gage favored the Americans in every dispute galled them; Gage's labors toward getting them quarters and rations were little appreciated. In truth, Gage gave them little personal attention. He might celebrate the Queen's birthday with a "royal salute" from his artillery and a parade, and organize a "Card Assembly" in hopes of discouraging gambling among the officers, but his only notice of Christmas was to have a deserter shot the day before.[1]

The army did grumble, gamble, and drink. In winter Boston

there was little else to do. Soldiers deserted; those that were caught were flogged or executed. Officers quarreled; one or two duels were aborted by sober comrades, and there were occasional court-martials. Cheap New England rum ignited street brawls. Some disapproving Americans considered it tremendously sinful, at least for propaganda purposes. (Others happily sold the rum.) By the standards of a European garrison town, however, all this was rather small beer. Many of the British went to church on Sunday mornings, at half-past eight, so as not to interfere with the regular congregation. And a lieutenant could comment in mid-February "Nothing has happened lately, this Town amazingly dull notwithstanding there are so many Regts. in it."[2]

The typical British regiment of Foot (infantry) consisted of a small regimental staff and a single battalion of ten companies. (It was termed a "regiment" or "battalion" indifferently, the first usually being used in reference to its administrative functions, the second concerning its tactical employment.) Of its ten companies, two—one of grenadiers and one of light infantry—were "flank," or elite, units. The remaining eight were termed "battalion companies." Each company had a drummer (some light infantry companies excepted) for signals and marching.

Grenadiers were selected from the tallest and strongest men in the regiment. Their characteristic headgear—a tall, pointed cap of fur or cloth—made them even more imposing. When a regiment formed in line, its grenadier company always had the traditional place of honor on its right flank; in action, it led the attack.

Light infantry were intended for scouting, skirmishing, and raiding. In its European wars, England had relied on German auxiliaries for such work. These being unavailable in North America, and the average provincial soldier unfit for such missions, the British had formed light infantry units out of their own regiments, from ". . such as have been most accustomed to the woods . . . good marksmen . . . active marchers . . . expert in firing ball . . . alert spirited soldiers able to endure fatigue."[3] This light infantry had been highly successful, and one company in each regiment was so trained and equipped. After the peace of 1763, however, these light companies tended to vanish—apparently some colonels felt that their different dress (varying by regiment, but typically short jackets and smart caps) spoiled the uniformity of their regiments on parade. They were officially reintroduced during a war scare in 1771 and their distinctive uniforms reappeared in even greater variety, but there was a decided lag in developing an effective system of training for them. Only in 1774 was Major General William Howe entrusted with the development of new maneuvers. It is difficult to determine how much (if any) specialized training Gage's light infantry had received. Gage's correspondence shows slight interest in such matters, and it may be that his order of 15 April 1775 that "The Grenadiers and Light Infantry in order to learn Grenadrs. Exercise and new evolutions are to be off duties . . ." actually may have been the first occasion this occurred.[4] Instead of drums (which would be awkward for irregular skirmishing) they tended to use some type of horn, the light company of the 4th Foot having ". . a German post-horn to give signals."[5]

British employment of these picked units apparently was influenced by long-standing Prussian practice. Once a campaign was about to open, they were detached from their parent regiments, and grouped into temporary battalions of grenadiers and light infantry. This gave the army commander an elite force for critical operations; Gage so employed them for the Lexington/Concord raid and for the intended main attack at Bunker's Hill. It also exposed them to heavy losses which had to be made up by skimming the tiny battalion companies of their best soldiers to keep the flank companies up to full strength. Captains of battalion companies naturally resented this, and there are frequent orders concerning their delays in furnishing replacements and their attempts to send "unfit" men.[6]

Each regiment also had several picked men designated as "pioneers." Equipped with axes, saws, spades, and picks, they functioned much as modern combat engineers, clearing obstacles from the front of advancing troops. In winter quarters they had the more prosaic detail of shovelling snow from walks and roads.

By late 1774, Gage had concentrated ten regiments—the 4th, 5th, 10th, 23d, 38th, 43d, 47th, 52d, 59th, and 64th—in Boston, plus a battalion of marines, an "Incorporated Corps" made up of detached companies from the 18th and 65th regiments, and four companies of artillery.[7] These regiments were considerably under their normal peace-time strength. (See Appendix IV) In the October 1774 muster of six regiments in Boston Gage had found only 1,766 effective enlisted men. Recruits were few and hard to secure, either in America or the British Isles. At the same time, disease and desertion cut considerably into Gage's force during the winter of 1774-1775. Also, there were accidental deaths, such as Private John McDonald of the 4th Foot who apparently drowned while drunk—and the unnamed sentry from the 10th who ". . jump'd off a Wharf . . . to save a Boy who had fallen over; he succeeded in his humane attempt, for which he paid with his life."[8] The official "returns" for this era are fragmentary and of doubtful accuracy, but by June 1775 the average regiment would have been lucky to put 300 effective enlisted men into action.

As Gage's situation worsened the British government ordered the 35th, 49th, and 63d Foot and the 17th Light Dragoon regiments to Boston, with an additional 500 drafts and recruits and 700 marines. French intelligence, which recently had infiltrated the British War Office and Admiralty, noted that special efforts were being made to bring these regiments up to at least their normal peace establishment of some 477 rank-and-file men.[9] These four regiments began coming into Boston on 11 June; by the 16th the light dragoons and the 63d Foot were all ashore, and the 35th and 49th were landing as their transports arrived. (Both regiments apparently had some elements still at sea on the 17th.) Their grenadier and light infantry companies were detached on arrival. The light dragoons had lost ". . . but 16 Horses on the Voyage" (which seemingly was considered good management) and the rest of their mounts would need some time ashore to be fully serviceable. Known as the "Death or Glory Boys" from the insignia—a skull-and-crossbones with the motto "Or glory" on their red-plumed helmets—the 17th Light Dragoons were an unusually smart regiment, but they would become a vile legend in Boston after they converted the Old South Meetinghouse into a riding hall.

The marines, recruits, and officer replacements had come in dribbles since 23 May. With the latter was Lieutenant Williams, dreaming after an uncomfortable voyage of ". . a Loin of Veal & lemon sauce." His introduction to the grim realities of beleaguered Boston was quick—". . salt Pork & pease . . ." Gage acknowledged the arrival of only 422 of the promised 500 recruits. Part of them, at least, were sent out to Castle William ". . to be cloathed and made ready . . ." On 14 June Gage ordered that all recruits be trained in individual marksmanship, but it was the afternoon of 16 June before the regiments "drew" for their respective share of them. It is doubtful that these men were of much service the next day.[10]

Four more infantry regiments were ordered to Boston in February, but their destination later was changed to New York where—

because of that city's greater strategic importance—the British had hoped to maintain a beach head. Anxious to divert them to Boston, Gage again asked Graves' help, and the admiral sent the *Mercury* to lay off New York and give the transport commanders their new orders. These troops, however, did not reach Boston until late June and early July.

The marines in Gage's army were a symptom of England's unpreparedness. In the first rush to reinforce Boston, for lack of sufficient soldiers, the marines at the various naval bases had been collected and shipped out aboard the *Somerset*, *Boyne*, and *Asia* (See Chapter III) with the hope of providing a ". . battalion of close to 600 men." Such was the haste that they were not issued gaiters or watchcoats: Their camp equipment, tents, and spare clothing were sent afterward by a ship bound for the West Indies which dropped them off at Rhode Island. On arrival, there proved to be less than 400 of them. Major John Pitcairn, their battalion commander, reported himself ". . a good deal hurt and mortified to find the marines so much shorter than the men are in the [Army] regiments . . ." and recommended that no more men under 5 feet, 6 inches tall be accepted. The marines' status produced an inter-service dispute. His own ships' complements of marines being below strength, Graves was reluctant to let them go; he did keep fifty of their best men, but loaned Pitcairn some lieutenants and sergeants to help drill and discipline his provisional battalion. Eventually the marines were quartered ashore, put on Army footing for pay and rations, and properly outfitted. Their organization was the same as that of an Army regiment, complete with a grenadier and a light infantry company. Pitcairn was a painstaking officer who ". . lived almost day and night amongst the men in their barracks for these five or six weeks past, on purpose to keep them from that pernicious rum . . ." He also drilled them hard, took them on practice marches into the countryside, and thoroughly won their roughneck devotion. There was one final brawl when Graves attempted to levy on Pitcairn for an additional fifty men to fill up the *Asia*'s marine detachment before it sailed for New York. The admiral's language was unrestrained, but Pitcairn gave back a polite refusal.[11]

This battalion—Lieutenant Frederick Mackenzie recorded it as having 336 effective rank-and-file on 12 March—was part of Percy's relief force at Lexington/Concord and had a total of seventy-four casualties. The promised reinforcements supposedly mustered 717 officers and men on embarkation; on its arrival in May, Pitcairn reorganized the whole force as the 1st and 2d Marine battalions.[12]

Together, all these troops (allowing for the fact that part of the 35th and 49th Foot still had not landed) must have amounted to approximately 6,000 effective rank-and-file, with several hundred more sick, wounded, or on special duties on the morning of 17 June. However, these were not the only personnel to eat the King's rations in Boston. Every regiment had its draggletail complement of "women"—the enlisted men's wives, whether legal or temporary. As a result, there also were children. (The Royal Artillery tended to be pre-eminent in both categories: in March 1776 at Boston, 390 artillerymen had 121 women and 123 children on their strength.) These were a rough-and-ready crew, a fruitful source of trouble whose misdeeds constantly enliven the order books. They bootlegged liquor, misappropriated blankets, and looted. They also mended, washed, and cooked for their man and his messmates; in emergencies, they worked in the hospitals. Some regimental commanders tried to ignore them; a few, like Percy, considered them part of their commands and looked after them. (Percy spent his own money to bring the 5th Foot's women and children to America, and made provision for those widowed and orphaned.) Now, with food scarce and very expensive, Gage had the good sense and humanity to allow ". . half a ration of provisions to every Soldier's Wife, and one quarter of a ration to every Soldier's Child."[13]

Food—along with forage and firewood—was not the least of Gage's worries. As early as 18 January the Army was put on salt provisions four days out of every week, the marines and regimental hospitals excepted; by early April fresh meat no longer could be obtained from the usual American sources. Knowing that a steady diet of salted meat was injurious to the troops' health and morale, Gage tried to secure fresh meat, flour, and oats from Canada. Graves' ships raided outlying islands for livestock and intercepted American ships loaded with foodstuffs. Both had only limited success. Army officers grumbled at the Navy's failure to secure more fresh meat, never considering the predicament of a small landing party attempting to steal sheep with several hundred angry farmers and fishermen in hot pursuit. Transports were sent to Nova Scotia for hay and coal, but it soon was obvious that Boston would have to be supplied direct from England.[14]

During the Seven Years' War in Europe, British artillery had won an outstanding reputation for aggressiveness and accuracy.[15] These qualities, naturally, had declined during the penny-pinching period of peace that followed. In 1775 Gage had only four companies, all from the 4th Battalion, Royal Artillery, in Boston.[16] All were far below strength, and two of their captains were—and remained—on leave. Gage fleshed them out with some 180 non-commissioned officers and privates from the infantry regiments. Artillerymen would load, lay, and fire the guns; the infantry "drafts" could pass ammunition, shift the trails, and haul and manhandle the guns into action. (Artillery of this period still employed hired civilian drivers who were apt to disappear at critical moments; therefore, once in combat, field guns usually were shifted by manpower.) These details put a considerable strain on Gage's small infantry regiments, and their commanders would not have detailed their better men—a natural reaction, but one which possibly contributed to the artillery's foul-up at Bunker's Hill. And, to rather add insult to injury, the infantry also had to provide the guards for the Artillery Park."[17] Even so, these four companies had hard cores of officers and men who were thoroughly professional gunners.

Gage's Artillery Park—". . . the grand depot of guns, ammunition, and stores . . ."[18]—was adequately equipped, including cannon up to 24-pounder siege guns. (Unlike modern artillery, a company of Royal Artillery of this period had no permanently assigned cannon, but manned whatever pieces the situation was adjudged to require.) Batteries were erected at the Boston Neck and at various points around the perimeter of the Boston peninsula. As previously noted, Gage also had taken over the "Admiral's Battery" on Copp's Hill and emplaced several 24-pounders there.

This artillery was commanded by Colonel Samuel Cleaveland who had a small staff, including the usual civilian commissaries, storekeepers, conductors, and clerks. As was customary for that period, he also functioned as the army's ordnance officer, responsible for the storage, issue and repair of its arms and ammunition. From what contemporary evidence exists, he was not competent. One anonymous account of Bunker's Hill blamed the artillery's failings there on Cleaveland's ". . dotage . . . spends his whole time dallying with the schoolmaster's daughters. God knows, he is old enough—he is no Sampson—yet he must have his Delilah."[19] But there was earlier evidence: during Lexington/Concord ". . our great commander of Artillery . . ." had sent the two guns attached to Percy's relief column (which were a major factor in Percy's successful withdrawal) off with only seven rounds apiece.[20] Incompetent he would remain; when the British abandoned Boston in 1776, he bollixed the evacuation of the army's artillery, leaving guns and ammunition behind for the needy Continentals.[21]

An odd weakness of the British Army was its lack of an effective military engineer service. The "Engineers" (they would not be "Royal" until 1787) consisted of something less than a hundred officers, assigned singly or in two's and three's to the various headquarters and fortresses throughout England and her overseas possessions. Except for a local company of semi-military workmen at Gibralter, there was nothing resembling engineer troops.[22] Gage had just one Engineer, Lieutenant John Montresor, with a handful of civilian artificers. Montresor had no formal training except what he got from his Engineer father, James Montresor, as a boy. Sent to America at eighteen as an infantry ensign and Engineer with General Braddock in 1754, he built frontier forts and docks, carried out wilderness explorations, and made excellent maps. However, his character had a touch of the fantastic—his *Journals* are spiked with wild claims and constant complaints of neglect, unrewarded sacrifices, and malicious persecution.[23] Certainly his performance was uneven: After Lexington/Concord he was quick to begin the fortification of the Charlestown Neck, but Mackenzie and Major General Henry Clinton both noted that he had not reconnoitered the area around Boston, and had not prepared or collected any maps of it. Consequently, the British could have little idea of the terrain difficulties they would encounter on the Charlestown Peninsula on 17 June.

For the fortification of Boston some infantry officers temporarily were appointed "assistant engineers." Mackenzie sourly noted that most of them hardly knew the names of the different parts of a defensive position, and were laughed at for their ignorance; Barker that ".. most of 'em [were] of no other use but just to keep the men at work, for which they get the name of Drivers ..." Captain George Harris of the 5th Foot, however, could jest about "his" fortification of which he was ".. not only planner and director, but partly executor." Harris often worked among his grenadiers who ".. fly to execute that for me which for others would be done with very bad grace." Infantry officer volunteers also were entrusted with the reconnaissance of the roads outside Boston (See Chapter II). The actual labor of building fortifications was performed by hired civilians or details of soldiers; the latter were supposed to receive extra pay and rum when so employed. As an example of his "paltry Oeconomy," Gage got the idea of having soldiers already assigned to guard duty ".. work for nothing ..." though they would be wearing their best uniforms. There were strong objections, and Gage returned to the traditional system.[24]

Gage, in stark contrast to Ward, had a complete staff of experienced officers. In theory, his army should have run like clockwork; in practice, his staff shared their general's nonchalance. Orders were issued, but staff officers never checked on their delivery or supervised their execution. The Lexington/Concord expedition had come near to complete disaster for that reason, but there was no reformation. On 5 June when the provisional battalions of grenadiers and light infantry were to set up their separate camp ".. they found nothing settled, no ground marked out for them, nor was there anybody ... to show them where to encamp; after waiting a considerable time, we set about pitching the Tents as we cou'd settle ourselves ... the whole was not finished till 6 or 7 o'clock, and after all it was then wrong and we must have to move again ... Everything still of a Piece!" Gage's staff was equally careless in its relations with its superiors. In England, Treasury officials protested the lack of reports as to the Army's

requirements for food and forage, without which they could not schedule their purchases or arrange for the necessary shipping except by guesswork. Their protests were ignored.[25]

The nature of Gage's intelligence system remains obscure. Despite his complaints (See Chapter II) of a lack of spies and information, he certainly had several well-placed sympathizers, including Dr. Benjamin Church of the Massachusetts Committee of Safety, and received frequent reports on American military dispositions and political developments. To date, however, there is no evidence that he made any effort to establish a methodical intelligence network. Though the Colonial office in London urged him to secure more information, it is doubtful that Gage bothered to forward all he did receive. He may have been somewhat short of money to pay spies, but there were loyalists in New England—such as those who sheltered Captain William Browne and Lieutenant Henry de Berniere during their road reconnaissance in March—who were willing to risk their necks for their King. Seemingly it was not too difficult to get information into Boston, just as American spies had little trouble getting it out. (If Captain Montresor can be believed, Gage had ".. all his Cabinet papers, Ministers' Letters, &, and his Correspondence all stole out of a large Closet, or Wardrobe, up one pair of Stairs on the Landing at the Government House at Boston ... 1775.") Gage was warned on 13 May of the American plans to occupy both Bunker's Hill and Dorchester Heights, but did nothing.[26]

In battle, the British infantry trusted to tightly controlled, short-range musketry—crushing volleys like those that gutted the enemy line at Minden and Quebec and wrecked the French Guard at Fontenoy—followed by a bayonet charge to clinch the victory. It was carefully schooled in such "firings," with emphasis on quick reloading and obedience to the word of command. But service against French and Indians in North America had taught it the value of aimed fire at individual targets, and Gage's army was so trained. As Mackenzie wrote on 15 January "The Regiments are frequently practiced at firing with ball at marks ... Premiums are sometimes given for the best Shots, by which means some of our men have become excellent marksmen." Mackenzie's regiment, the 23d Foot, was quartered on a Boston wharf, and had set up ".. figures of men as large as life ..." on small rafts out in the harbor for realistic targets.

A British recruit might not have been as familiar with firearms as his American counterpart, but—once enlisted—he certainly received more training, both in unit and individual shooting. Despite dear legends, he could be as good a shot as his American opponent. Moreover, the fact that he had a bayonet, and was taught how to use it, gave him confidence in hand-to-hand fighting. The major problem, however, was well stated by Lieutenant Williams ".. most of our Regt. here being composed of recruits and Drafts, who never having seen service, foolishly imagine that when danger is feard they secure themselves by discharging their muskets, with or without aim. ... Theory is nothing without practice, & it requires one Campaign at least, to make a good soldier." At Lexington/Concord even the light infantry and grenadiers had been ".. so wild and irregular there was no keeping them in any order ... ;" they had fired blindly, sometimes hitting their comrades, and left their ranks to plunder.[27]

The average British private was as young and untried as the American volunteers he faced. Though better equipped and armed, he had not yet been completely trained or disciplined. Most of the junior officers were as raw as the men they commanded.

Certain strengths the English had. Their senior officers were veterans of the great wars, mostly competent and entirely brave; every regiment had a hard cadre of tested sergeants. Beyond that were the regiments themselves—living institutions, many of them generations old, each with its established hierarchy of command, its separate history and the traditions embodied in its title, badge, and colors. And the men themselves held the contemptuous assurance that they were Englishmen.

CHAPTER VI
THE COMING OF THE MAJOR GENERALS

While the Americans formed their new army, hoping that Gage would not strike until it was in some sort of order, Gage kept behind his fortifications, fearful that Ward was about to attack him—and that the Bostonians would seize that opportunity to break out in revolt. Against the first of these imagined dangers he mounted reinforced guards, kept his whole force on constant alert, and rushed the construction of additional fortifications. (Men on the construction details had their daily allowance of rum increased to two gills.) His second bugbear took care of itself: now that actual hostilities had begun, most of the Patriot element of the Boston population wanted to get out of town.

After some sub rosa haggling, it was agreed that those Bostonians who wished to depart were to deposit their weapons and ammunition with the city's Selectmen; they then would be allowed to ". . remove out of the town with their effects." The Massachusetts Provincial Congress promptly granted a like permission to such Loyalists ". . as should incline thereto . . ." to move into Boston. For some time, wagons passed in and out of the city as thousands of civilians made their choice of allegiance. The Loyalists were comparatively few, but often families of wealth, status, and influence which suddenly had found themselves refugees. Frightened and resentful, they began to assail Gage for his leniency. Once all the "rebels" had departed, these Loyalists clamored, Ward would be free to bombard Boston. Whether entirely because of this pressure or not, Gage soon began welshing on his agreement. First, he ruled that no food, medicines, or merchandise could be taken out of the city; passes to leave became harder to secure. But the Patriot element continued to go anyway, and the Provincial Congress replied by ordering Ward to allow Loyalists to take nothing but clothing and furniture into Boston. Gage then forbade any male over sixteen years old to leave, though women and children might continue to do so. The agreement collapsed completely. A considerable number of rebellious-minded citizens were left in Boston, but Gage had their guns. "I fancy this will quiet him a little . . ." observed irreverent Lieutenant Barker of the 4th Foot. Gage overlooked the fact that these interned Bostonians still had their wits, their eyes and ears, and their angers—and that they thus strengthened the American intelligence network.[1]

The Loyalist refugees were a further drain on Boston's precarious food supply. Some of them could be employed as civilian officials in the local administration, but there was no recorded effort to make soldiers out of them until the following November. Then, three companies of "Loyal American Associators" were formed under one Timothy Ruggles (given the much inflated title of "Brigadier" for that purpose) for interior security duty.[2]

Meanwhile the American command shook itself down. Ward took post at Cambridge with most of the Massachusetts troops, stationing Thomas with the rest of them at Roxbury, where the Rhode Island army gradually joined him. Stark's and Reed's New Hampshire regiments were sent to the Medford area, north of Cambridge; the Connecticut troops were divided between Roxbury and Cambridge. There were repeated rumors of imminent British attack: On 29 April the Committee of Safety voted that the neighboring towns send half of their militia ". . immediately to Roxbury and Cambridge, as a reenforcement to our army, and that the rest of the inhabitants hold themselves in readiness to march at a minute's warning."[3] There was another alarm during 8-10 May that the British were planning to occupy the Dorchester peninsula and attack Roxbury. The Provincial Congress considered evacuating Cambridge and sending the army's artillery and stores into the interior, but Ward and most of his officers agreed that their proper course of action was to call up all available militia and minute men and seize the Dorchester area first. Thomas, however, opposed such action until the army had proper artillery and artillerymen, and someone competent to lay out "Regular Intrenchments."[4] Thomas apparently held himself somewhat independent of Ward, and seems not to have attended the Council of War regularly. His camp was described as having a far more military air—". . spirited, active, regular and clean . . ."—than Ward's, but he made no effort to fortify it, even though it was far more exposed to attack than Cambridge.[5]

Israel Putnam's long experience had taught him that soldiers were happier and better behaved if kept busy. He quickly had all the Connecticut troops around Cambridge at work with picks and shovels when they were not drilling, building three small forts. (Probably these American fatigue parties also got extra rum: They definitely were turned out early enough to attend morning prayers before work.) Forts "Number One" and "Number Two" were on the Charles River, guarding the bridge that was the only direct link between Cambridge and Roxbury. (As part of the Lexington/Concord expedition, at least one armed British tender successfully had worked its way well up the Charles River.)[6] "Number Three" blocked the roads leading into Cambridge from the Charlestown Neck and Lechmere Farm. Lechmere Farm was the point the British had landed during the night of 18-19 April for their raid on Concord.) That done, he began trying to stir up some excitement.

On the afternoon of 13 May Putnam marched what a British officer estimated as ". . between 2 and 3,000 of the Rebels . . ." across Charlestown Neck and over Bunker's Hill to Breed's Hill "where they kept parading for a long time." The *Somerset* still was anchored in the ferry way between Boston and Charlestown; she beat to quarters and cleared for action. The Americans broke off their drill and came swinging downhill through Charlestown. Behind the thirty-two heavy guns of the *Somerset*'s broadside, eager gunners poised their matches; marines on the quarterdeck and in the tops checked their muskets' priming. One shot from that American column and it—with most of Charlestown to boot—would be blasted. But American discipline (and, undoubtedly, prudence) held firm. The column saluted the *Somerset* with nothing deadlier than a derisive "War-hoop," and headed back across Bunker's Hill.[7]

Sometime during May the inhabitants of Charlestown quietly evacuated their homes and moved inland, leaving the place empty except for occasional American patrols. Nobody seems to have noted and recorded their going. If any of them still were there during Putnam's demonstration, they probably left immediately.

For a few days in Boston there was relative quiet except for a bad fire on 17 May which burned up one entire wharf area, along with the arms and clothing of the 65th Foot and those of four companies of the 47th. Amid this calm, a joint committee from the Committee of Safety and the Council of War had been appointed to reconnoiter ". . the high lands of Cambridge and Charlestown." On the 12th this committee reported to the Committee of Safety, recommending that the approaches to Cambridge be fortified and that ". . a strong redoubt be raised on Bunker's Hill, with cannon planted there, to annoy the enemy coming out of Charlestown, also to annoy them going by water [the Mystic River] to Medford." The Committee of Safety felt this recommendation was beyond its expertise, and so passed it to the Council of War; the Council, in turn, could reach no agreement and the idea was shelved for the time being. Dr. Benjamin Church had been the subcommittee's chairman, so Gage soon knew about their deliberations.[8]

Gage had a new adjutant general recently arrived from England, Lieutenant Colonel James Abercrombie, an adventuresome Scot who had served with Putnam and Rogers—and found John Stark cross-grained and insubordinate. Early on 18 May he went reconnoitering up the Charles River in a man-of-war's boat and rowed into an American ambush. Nobody was hit but the boat was riddled; Abercrombie's party apparently had to bail constantly to keep it afloat till they reached safety. This was the first British attempt at reconnaissance since Lexington/Concord, and the last one before Bunker's Hill.[9]

While gathering reinforcements for Gage, the British government had included three major generals. With a larger force, Gage would require subordinates of that grade. Moreover, because Gage had no reputation as a fighting general (Amherst, who now held the important post of Lieutenant General of the Ordnance, undoubtedly remembered La Galette), these must be aggressive combat officers. The three selected certainly had won that reputation, and also represented an excellent variety of talent and experience.

William Howe, the senior, was considered England's best light infantry officer. He had been at the second taking of Louisbourg in 1758; the next year he had commanded the light infantry who cleared Wolfe's way to the Plains of Abraham; in 1761 he served with credit in the capture of Belle-Ile, off the northwest coast of France; and in 1762 he took part in the capture of Havana "When the Moro low was laid." A tall man, very military in his bearing, absolutely courageous, kindly, and fond of good living, Howe was popular with his troops. He was an excellent tactician, a capable strategist, and thoroughly experienced in amphibious warfare. Time would prove that he lacked the energy and intellectual grasp necessary to a commander in chief; though he never lost a battle, he seldom exploited his successes.[10]

Henry Clinton was the youngest of the three, a short, plumpish, unimpressive officer. Most of his service had been in northern Germany under Prince Ferdinand of Brunswick; educated in this semi-Prussian school of warfare, he tended to look down on American experience such as Howe's. Clinton was a difficult subordinate—always eager and active, full of unsolicited good advice, forever ready to point out the flaws in his commander's plan. He possessed a furious bravery and considerable tactical skill and daring, but was cursed with an extreme sensitivity that could not abide the least criticism, and tortured him with suspicions of enmity and insult where none existed. This last characteristic was merely the outward evidence of a fragile mind: A few years previously his wife's death had left him shattered for months; his general conduct—or possibly its contrast to his prosaic everyday appearance—still could disturb his associates—"Wild to a degree and leaky as a sieve, with all the appearance of Mystery."[11] Alone of the three, Clinton wrote the story of his American campaigns: *The American Rebellion: Sir Henry Clinton's Narrative of His Campaigns, 1775-1782.* (A comparatively moderate statement of history as he saw it, it involved him in more controversy.) He also left reams of notes and documents—often undated, frequently almost illegible—justifying and glorifying his every act. How much of this had a factual basis, how much was defensive fantasy never can be known.

John Burgoyne was the oldest, the junior-ranking, and the most complex of the three—a big, handsome man of more ambition than capacity, a gamester, a fond husband, a man-about-town, and a successful minor playwright. In action he was fearless, with a showy leadership that mocked all dangers. He had achieved fame as a colonel of light dragoons in Portugal in 1762, at the head of a regiment he had organized and trained according to his own convictions—that enlisted men be treated as fellow humans as well as fellow soldiers, that young officers must master every skill of their profession and complete their educations, that horses required care and training. To his soldiers he was "Gentleman Johnny," their friend and protector, a man to admire and follow.[12]

These three officers had become major generals in 1772, and therefore had seen no active service in that grade. Apparently Burgoyne was the only one ever to have fought an independent action of any size—the capture of Valentia d'Alcantara from the Spaniards by a well-managed cavalry raid. Their coming, especially Howe's, was eagerly awaited by the troops in Boston. However, their arrival on 25 May changed nothing; they would have no commands until Gage saw fit to assign them.[13] Until then they could do little but settle themselves in and study the tactical situation, which was plain enough. As Burgoyne put it, the army needed "elbow room"—a phrase that later boomeranged against him—but did express their mutual feelings.[14]

Several of the islands in Boston harbor—especially Noddle's and Hog islands at its north end—were traditional pasture and hayfield areas. Over a thousand head of livestock still were grazing on them in May, apparently the property of American farmers on the mainland. These would have been an invaluable supplement to the salt rations of the British troops, but for some reason Gage—who then was attempting to get fresh meat from Canada—had made no effort to secure them. Finally, on 20 May, a lieutenant and thirty men were sent in an unarmed sloop to Grape Island (off Hingham, approximately nine miles southeast of Boston) to collect hay for the army's horses. Thomas soon learned of their presence. After some fruitless long-range shooting from the mainland, he found boats for three companies and sent them over to the island. The British withdrew unhurt with some seven tons of hay; the equally undamaged Americans burned the rest of it on the island.[15]

Four days later, probably alerted by this skirmish, the Committee of Safety recommended that livestock and hay be removed from the harbor islands, particularly Noddle's and Hog.[16] Gage was warned of this decision the next day by his informants, and referred the problem to Graves. Graves (who had rented a building on Noddle's Island for storage of his small reserve of naval stores) increased his boat patrols, but observed that an army garrison on the islands would be much more effective in protecting the stock. Gage ignored his suggestion. On the afternoon of the 28th a detachment of Americans slipped across from mainland to Noddle's Island and began setting houses and hay barns on fire and ". . . Killing the Cows and Horses" they could not drive off easily. Graves landed his marines and sent the light schooner *Diana* (commanded by one of his nephews, Lieutenant Thomas Graves) to work in behind Noddle's Island and cut off the Americans. Gage's army, however, sat tight in Boston. "The General," Major Stephen Kemble, Gage's deputy-adjutant-general (and brother-in-law) observed primly, "by no means approved of the Admiral's scheme, supposing it to be a trap, which it proved to be." The Americans got away to Hog Island, wading across a tidal creek ". . up to their necks." Putnam brought several regiments and two field guns across the Mystic River and along the shore north of Noddle's Island to support them, wading out waist-deep into the bay for better shooting.

Until sundown there was a constant blaze of musket and artillery fire, with very little harm to either side. Then, wind and tide turning unfavorable, the *Diana* went aground near the Winnisimet ferry landing at the mouth of Mystic, within some sixty yards of Putnam's force; as the tide ebbed, she fell over on her beam ends (side) and could no longer use her guns. An attempt by several ships' boats to tow her off failed under heavy American fire, and the *Diana* had to be abandoned. One side or the other set her afire, but the Americans were able to salvage her four guns. Bickering—mostly at very long range—continued for several days as Graves got most of his supplies off Noddle's Island, with minimal assistance from Gage. He had two men killed and several wounded, most of them in the attempt to save the *Diana*; the Americans had four wounded and possibly one killed. Following this up, the Americans burned all the houses on Noddle's and Hog islands, and cleared all the livestock from Deer Island, at the mouth of the outer harbor, and Peddock's (or Pettick's) Island, just west of Hull in the southern end of the harbor. On 8—9 June Gage finally ordered 200 light infantry to Noddle's Island to secure hay: This amphibious operation was carried out smartly and met no resistance, but it was far too late. The Americans had burned off the island—". . there was a very small quantity of hay, and that so bad that its fit only for litter."[17]

These operations filled up the American commissary stores, and also the Americans' good opinion of themselves, Israel Putnam's most of all. Rumor put the British casualties on Noddle's Island at 300. Many American officers were eager to push the fighting, certain of further successes. But General Ward was pondering his army's ability to fight a major action. Its supply of ammunition was slim indeed, and Noddle's Island had been a major wasting of it. And the Massachusetts Committee of Supplies was worrying that ". . a great consumption by cannon may be ruinous on our side."[18]

CHAPTER VII
THE SAFETY OF THE COLONY

The *Cerberus* had brought more than the three major generals and the official announcement of Graves' promotion to Vice Admiral of the White. There also were instructions for Gage to declare Massachusetts in a state of rebellion and under the "Law Martial." This Gage did eventually on 12 June, offering ". . his Majesty's most gracious pardon to all who shall lay down their Arms, and return to the duties of peaceable Subjects"—with the exception of Samuel Adams and John Hancock whose offenses were adjudged ". . of too flagitious a nature to admit of any other consideration than that of condign punishment." For reasons unknown, Gage had Burgoyne prepare this proclamation: Burgoyne filled it with a purple rodomontade that produced much laughter but no repentence.[1]

One thing this proclamation did accomplish: American leaders were forewarned that Gage would, however reluctantly, follow it up with some offensive action. Ward of necessity had concentrated on organizing and equipping his army, but on 6 June he, Thomas, Spencer, and Heath had reconnoitered Dorchester Heights but again concluded that occupying this area would be too risky.[2] On 12 June Ward moved Reed's regiment into billets just west of the Charlestown Neck, with its outlying sentries on Bunker's Hill. Stark's oversize regiment was at Medford, some two miles to the

northwest. These two New Hampshire regiments, approximately 1,300 strong, formed Ward's left wing. His center, in and around Cambridge, consisted of fifteen Massachusetts infantry regiments, most of Gridley's Massachusetts artillery regiment, Putnam's Connecticut regiment, part of Spencer's Connecticut regiment, and Sargent's four New Hampshire companies, totalling approximately 9,000 officers and men. Ward's right flank—Thomas's command in and around Roxbury—had nine Massachusetts infantry regiments, most of Spencer's Connecticut regiment, Greene's Rhode Island contingent, and several companies of Gridley's artillery, possibly 6,000 officers and men. A considerable portion of Ward's army was not available for duty—the sick, men without weapons, men "on command" (assigned to special details). As a rough estimate, possibly as few as 5,000 out of the 6,083 Massachusetts rank and file around Cambridge were "present, fit for duty" on 17 June. Several regiments, especially Gridley's artillery, were not yet fully organized; Ward's staff had little concept of its duties, and the ammunition shortage continued acute. But if Gage moved, this army must fight, ready or not.[3]

During 13—15 June the British commanders worked out their plan for a coordinated attack, beginning on 18 June, to break the American lines. Dorchester Heights would be their first objective: These seized and fortified, the British would pinch out Roxbury by converging attacks across the Dorchester and Boston necks. After establishing a fortified outpost there, they would make an amphibious landing ". . with all we can muster . . ." on the Charlestown Peninsula and then drive the Americans from Cambridge. Executed with surprise, speed, and determination, this plan easily could have been successful.[4]

Boston was a poor town for secrets. From the first, their discussions—or perhaps over-confident after-dinner talk as the port was passed—were picked up by American agents. These probably were minor household servants or inconspicuous tradespeople. Another story is that a New Hampshire "gentleman of undoubted veracity" had overheard British officers talking some weeks earlier about what Gage was going to do once his reinforcements arrived; on returning home this veracious gentleman had told the New Hampshire Committee of Safety what he had learned, and the New Hampshire committee passed the information to their Massachusetts colleagues. Some rumor monger started the tale that Gage's American wife betrayed his plans. All that is certain is that the Massachusetts Committee of Safety learned of Gage's plan almost as quickly as it was developed.

On 15 June the Committee of Safety accordingly resolved: "Whereas, it appears of importance to the safety of this Colony, that possession of the hill called *Bunker's Hill*, in *Charlestown*, be securely kept and defended, and also some one hill or hills on *Dorchester Neck* be likewise secured; therefore

"*Resolved unanimously,* That it be recommended to the Council of War, that the above mentioned *Bunker's Hill* be maintained by sufficient force being posted there; and as the particular situation of *Dorchester Neck* is unknown to this Committee, they desire that the Council of War take and pursue such steps respecting the same as to them shall appear to be for the security of this Colony.

"*Ordered,* That Colonel *Benjamin White* and Colonel *Joseph Palmer* be a Committee to join with a Committee from the Council of War to proceed to *Roxbury* Camp, there to consult with the General Officers on matters of importance, and to communicate to them a Resolve this day passed in this Committee respecting *Bunker's Hill* in *Charlestown*, and *Dorchester Neck*."

All the militia were to hold themselves ready ". . to march on the shortest notice, completely equipped, having thirty rounds of cartridges per man." The 18th would be Sunday: therefore the people were to go ".. to meeting armed on *Lord's* day . . ." as in the desperate old times when Massachusetts fought for its life against the Indian.[5]

The Committee did its best to maintain secrecy concerning these deliberations. Apparently the order concerning Bunker's Hill and Dorchester Neck was not entered in its Journal until 19 June. Even so, it was only by accident that the Committee's decision was kept from Gage—by lucky coincidence, it had sent its trusted Dr. Church off to Philadelphia with dispatches for the Continental Congress in late May. Church had been vexed, but could not avoid the mission.[6]

Little can be said about the joint committee that went ".. to Roxbury camp, there to consult with the General officers . . ." Its purpose undoubtedly was to determine if Thomas was willing to forestall Gage's plan to seize Dorchester Heights. Thomas, however, remained unwilling, and his "council of war" (including Greene, Spencer, and Heath) seems to have supported his opinion. He may have begun some belated efforts to strengthen his position, but little—if anything—effective had been done by the morning of the 17th.

Ward convened his council of war at Cambridge on the 16th. No record or first-hand account of this meeting ever has been found. We do not know which officers were there, what opinions they offered, or even the exact decisions they reached. Apparently Thomas and his subordinates did not come over from Roxbury: Warren, Putnam, Gridley, and some regimental commanders attended, but it seems certain that Pomeroy was at home on leave for a rest.[7] As to their proceedings, we have only old tales. According to these, Ward opposed occupying Bunker's Hill for fear of bringing on a battle, citing their lack of ammunition and organization. Putnam is described as eager for action, arguing that the army would fight well enough behind entrenchments—"Americans [so somebody recalled his words] are not at all afraid of their heads, though very much afraid of their legs; if you cover these, they will fight forever." As for the shortage of ammunition, expert American marksmanship would ensure that almost every shot would drop its redcoat. The important thing was to make the British come out and fight. Colonel William Prescott (and probably other regimental commanders) supported him, and finally Warren agreed with them. Thus outvoted, Ward gave in and issued his orders. Colonel Prescott would march that night to occupy and entrench a position—supposedly Bunker's Hill—on the Charlestown Peninsula.[8]

The Charlestown Peninsula was a ham-shaped area, approximately one and one-quarter miles long, lying between the estuaries of the Charles and Mystic rivers. It was joined to the mainland by its narrow Neck which was only some thirty feet wide at high tide. The Neck's southern shore was protected by a tidal mill dam, built across the angle from the base of the peninsula to the mainland and backed by a large swampy mill pond. (This dam offered a precarious footpath for men moving in single file, but such use would be suicidal in daylight.)[9] Bunker's Hill rose across the narrow western end of the peninsula: Approximately 110 feet high, it dominated the Neck, the rest of the peninsula, and the mouth of the Mystic River. Any fortifications constructed there would be out of effective range of the British battery on Copp's Hill in Boston; British warships could not elevate their guns sufficiently to fire on them effectively. Occupation of Bunker's Hill thus would deny the British any real use of the Charlestown Peninsula, yet would not be a direct challenge to the British position in Boston. Troops stationed there could be reinforced or withdrawn with little risk.

Southeast of Bunker's Hill—to which it was connected by a low saddle—and directly behind the now-empty streets of Charlestown, Breed's Hill rose some sixty feet. It was comparatively isolated and easy to bypass, but it did command the northern end of Boston and its harbor. Consequently, the British would be certain to react strongly to its occupation by the Americans. Graves (See Chapter III) already had threatened to burn Charlestown if this occurred. Any American force stationed here would run the risk of being enveloped and cut off by British landings. And, while heavy artillery emplaced on Breed's Hill could batter northern Boston, it is doubtful that the Americans had a single reliable gun of sufficient caliber for that purpose. They certainly did not have enough ammunition for a bombardment. (Off in the northeastern tip of the Peninsula was the solitary thirty-five foot rise of Moulton's (or Morton's) Hill, too low and too distant to have any immediate military importance for the Americans.)

Ward's orders were oral and remain a mystery. The Committee of Safety had specified Bunker's Hill as the point to be occupied; its official report of 25 July stated that Breed's Hill was occupied ".. by some mistake." Yet Colonel Prescott later would write flatly, "On the 16th June, in the evening, I received orders to march to Breed's Hill."[10] This conflict never has been explained. It seems unlikely that Ward—after long considering Bunker's Hill too risky a venture—suddenly should have consented to the far riskier advance to Breed's Hill. Possibly the Council of War crowded him into accepting that gamble. Possibly Prescott misunderstood his orders. Possibly, at the urging of Putnam, he disobeyed them. Possibly Ward left the final decision to his subordinates. This was a very amateur army, somewhat toplofty over its recent small successes, and bored with inaction.

Certainly the force Ward assigned Prescott was sufficient for a large-scale fatigue detail, but much too weak for any independent operation. It consisted of 300 men of Prescott's own regiment, and parts of Colonel Ebenezer Bridge's and Colonel James Frye's regiments, the whole totaling "about one thousand men." (Frye being disabled by gout, Lieutenant Colonel James Brickett commanded the detail from his regiment.) To these Massachusetts troops were added 200 Connecticut men under Captain Thomas Knowlton from Putnam's regiment, and Captain Samuel Gridley's company of artillery with two light guns. Such a formation, taken from two different state contingents and four different regiments, would have little cohesion and be hard to control in action, but would do well enough for digging. The men were to carry their blankets and a day's rations. At six o'clock on the evening of the 16th, the men of the three Massachusetts regiments formed up on Cambridge common where the Reverend Samuel Langdon, president of Harvard College, offered a prolonged prayer for their success and safety. That and other essential preliminaries completed, they moved off at about nine, drums tapping through the thickening dark. Two sergeants with dark lanterns led the column, followed by Prescott and Colonel Richard Gridley, who—in his capacity as the army's engineer—was to lay out the fortifications. Down the road toward the Neck, Knowlton's Connecticut detachment fell in, followed by several wagons loaded with entrenching tools. Apparently Putnam was with Knowlton: In this peculiar army of allied sovereign colonies, a Connecticut brigadier general had no authority over a Massachusetts colonel, but Putnam was not likely to hang back on such an occasion because of military protocol. Only the senior officers knew their objective.[11]

Soon Prescott commanded silence in the ranks. The drums stopped, and men swallowed their expletives when they stumbled on the rough track. Once across the Neck, Prescott detached Captain John Nutting's company of his own regiment, reinforced by ten of Knowlton's men, to scout along the shore road and establish outposts in Charlestown.[12] Then, on the far slope of Bunker's Hill, he halted the column and briefed the officers as to their mission. Here again, we have only tradition—supposedly the result was a furious, complicated argument over whether they were to fortify Bunker's Hill or Breed's, with Gridley protesting that valuable time was being wasted. At last—so goes the story—it was decided that the principal fortification would be built on Breed's Hill and that a supporting position would be constructed later on Bunker's.[13] The column went on to Breed's Hill where Gridley hurriedly staked out the trace of a redoubt approximately "8 rods" (132 feet) square, with a small redan (triangular projection) on the side facing Charlestown and Boston. A narrow gorge (opening) was left on the opposite side to permit easy movement in and out of the redoubt.[14] Then the troops started digging. This was something they understood and they made the dirt fly with a speed no British fatigue detail could have equaled. It was almost midnight; first light—enough for the British to see and shoot by— would be about four o'clock the next morning. Below them, starlight showed British warships swinging at anchor; ships' bells measured the dwindling time, and guard boats rowed their constant patrols. In Charlestown, Nutting's men could hear the faint challenges of British sentinels in Boston. Putnam (if he actually had accompanied the column) went back to his headquarters near Cambridge.[15]

Understandably Prescott worried, though he allowed no evidence of it to show. A British attack or bombardment would catch his raw troops unprotected and scattered at their work. His command was completely isolated, the nearest Americans being Reed's regiment to the west of the Neck. Detaching another company to patrol the Boston side of the peninsula, he kept the rest digging. The redoubt must be complete enough to give them shelter by first light; also, the harder they worked, the less time they would have for worry.

William Prescott stood over six feet tall and powerfully built—a calm, unhurried, strong-minded man with an innate authority. While still in his teens he had served bravely during the first capture of Louisbourg in 1745, but this seems to have been the total of his active experience. He was not a professional citizen-soldier, eager for military service and distinction like Stark, Putnam, and Knowlton; in place of experience and professional skill, he could offer only determination, courage, and devotion. His account of the coming battle has curious lapses but makes it plain that he did not suffer fools gladly—or exactly trust those foreigners from Connecticut—but to his regiment he was "our own Colonel Prescott."

Luck was with him. Among Clinton's miscellaneous papers is one stating that he had been reconnoitering on the evening of the 16th (he did not record where) and thought he saw American activity (type not specified) on the Charlestown Peninsula. He therefore submitted a written recommendation that the Dorchester operation be dropped in favor of an immediate landing on the Charlestown ". . side . . . if we were of active disposition we should be landed by tomorrow morning at daybrake." Howe agreed with him, but Gage ". . seemed to doubt their intention . . ." and would do nothing. Howe wrote back to England, "As a specimen of our knowledge of Service [i.e. the way this army of Gage's operates], the Centrys on the Boston side had heard the Rebels at work all night, without making any other report of it, except mentioning it in Conversation in the Morning."[16]

CHAPTER VIII
THE TEN OLDEST COMPANIES

Captain Thomas Bishop of His Majesty's sloop-of-war *Lively*, 20 guns, now at anchor in the *Somerset*'s former place in the Boston-Charlestown ferry way, had faced a court-martial on 5 June. The charge was "deliberate neglect of duty" over the disposition of money and goods from a wrecked Spanish ship: The court's finding was "guilty," though only of unintentional neglect. Bishop was sentenced to receive an official reprimand—a punishment Admiral Graves administered with gusto.[1] It may be assumed that the *Lively* was now a very taut ship. When "at 4 AM" its lookout saw ". . Rebels throwing up a redoubt" on Breed's Hill, Bishop at once beat to quarters and opened fire.[2] Gage awoke to find his plans for seizing Dorchester Heights on 18 June capsized, and a sudden new problem lowering at him from Breed's Hill.

For the captain of the 20-gun sloop-of-war *Glasgow*, moored in the deepest part of the channel through the Back Bay, it was simple enough. At 4:30 AM he lowered a boat to carry his stream (stern) anchor out from the side of his ship and drop it at a suitable distance; then, by heaving in its cable, he swung the *Glasgow* ". . Broad Side to Charles Town Neck . . . fired several Guns at the Redout." By 9:00 AM the Copp's Hill battery was firing occasionally ". . with Shott & Shells." This shooting seems to have been slow and methodical, the gunners firing only when they had a definite target.

June 17th was a pleasant day in most respects—dry and clear, with light breezes and low humidity. The temperatures would climb from around 64° to a little above 80° by midafternoon. (It probably seemed far hotter in the cramped, dusty redoubt on Breed's Hill, and there soon was a tradition that the battle ". . was fought on one of the hottest days ever known in the country.") But to Graves and his captains, this weather was far from ideal: those fresh breezes were insufficient for their bigger ships—and even worse, they were blowing out of the west and were broken by periods of flat calm. Ship handling in Boston harbor was going to be a tricky, back-breaking business for understrength crews that also must man the guns and the ships' boats.[3]

Gage summoned his principal subordinates for a hasty conference—Howe, Clinton and Burgoyne, with the brigadiers Percy, Robert Pigot, and Valentine Jones and various staff officers.[4] Graves spoke for his squadron. This meeting has been second-guessed by a long succession of historians, mostly without military education or experience. We should remember that these officers were experienced professionals of much and varied service: They dealt with hard factors of troop strengths, terrain, weather, time, wind and tide, the number of boats available to move troops, and what they could know of their enemy.

The Americans toiling around the half-finished redoubt on Breed's Hill were both a threat and an opportunity. If allowed to consolidate their position on the Charlestown Peninsula and to emplace heavy guns there, they probably could make Boston untenable for the British. However, these Americans on Breed's Hill appeared to be isolated, their defenses incomplete: A prompt counterattack should round up the lot of them, and might open a chance of breaking up the Yankee army. Everyone present agreed that, in Howe's words, ". . they must be removed from thence as soon as the troops and the boats could be got in readiness for that purpose." The only question was where and how to attack.

This would be an amphibious operation. Accordingly, the

primary consideration would be the number and capacity of the boats available for landing troops. There were ". . none of our old accustomed flat boats . . ." which the British had used so successfully during the Seven Years' War; instead, it would be necessary to employ ordinary ships' boats, collected from the men-of-war and transports all around the harbor, from the Back Bay to Castle William.[5] These would be a mixed lot, some in poor condition and indifferently manned, none of them designed for landing operations or transporting field guns. (See Graves' comments, Chapter III.) Their capacity would be only some 1,100 rank and file, out of the 1,600 to 2,200 men (plus artillery) the British generals judged necessary for this mission. Consequently, two round trips would be required.

The landing therefore would have to be made at a point near enough to Boston to permit the second wave of troops to land before their first wave might get into difficulties with superior American forces. Also, it was essential that both waves be landed in that comparatively short period when the tide was running full (so the boats could come right up to the beach to unload) and before it began to ebb. "Full sea" (high tide) would be at 2:50 PM.[6] Finally, the landing site must be an area where field artillery could be gotten ashore easily, and where warships could stand in close enough to provide effective fire support.

Today, a look at the map suggests that it would have been simple to send a force up the Mystic River and seize the Charlestown Neck, thus neatly bagging Prescott's command and cutting off its reinforcements at one blow. However, the time and space factors just mentioned made such a move impractical. The Americans might have strong reserves around Bunker's Hill; if not, they certainly could march reinforcements in from Medford and Cambridge faster than the British could bring theirs by boat. Though, theoretically, a shallow-draft warship—such as the *Symmetry* or the *Spitfire*—could anchor in close to the northern side of the Neck and sweep it with its guns, those light western breezes would make it difficult for the ship to get up the Mystic, even with the help of the rising tide. If boats were told off to tow it into position, few would be left to transport the landing force. Abercrombie's experience, and the failure to tow the *Diana* clear, would suggest that any such effort might be a costly failure. Also, there was the awkward fact that the Mystic River never had been "sounded" to determine the location and depth of its main channel; any ship venturing in would run the risk of going aground like the *Diana*. Possibly Graves had been negligent in not charting the Mystic in April when he had sounded the Charles River—but the Mystic wasn't much of a river and went nowhere in particular.[7]

Since the western shores of the Back Bay were edged with swamps and mud flats, landing there would be impossible against any serious resistance. The Americans were known to have considerable forces around Lechmere Point to oppose any such effort.[8] As previously noted, the southern side of the Charlestown Neck was inaccessible because of the mill dam and the marshy pond behind it.

A landing on the Charlestown wharves facing Boston could be supported by the Copp's Hill battery and naval gunfire, but it would be directly under the American redoubt. If there were Americans in Charlestown, it would involve street fighting—a slow, messy type of combat in which the superior organization and maneuverability of the British troops would be wasted.[9]

On the northeastern corner of the peninsula, called Moulton's (sometimes Morton's) Point, a roadway of sorts came down to the beach and the shore was open, easy, and level. This was farther from Boston than the Charlestown wharves, but out of effective range of the redoubt. A landing here could be given naval support.

Most of what we know of this British council of war comes from Clinton's egocentric account, which is not too clear and may contain as much hindsight as foresight. His story is that he wanted to land immediately with 500 men to seize a position at the ". . Jew's burying ground . . . where he would have been in perfect security and within half gun shot of the narrow neck of communication of the Rebels . . . the redoubt was incomplete no flanks, neither picketted pallasaded or ditched."[10] Howe meanwhile could make the main landing elsewhere with whatever boats remained, catching the Americans between them. There is no evidence that Clinton ever had been on the Charlestown Peninsula, or had any knowledge of its terrain. The "Jew's burying ground" has not been identified, but it must have been fairly near Charlestown—which suggests that Clinton planned to land on the southern side of the peninsula, between the mill dam and Charlestown. Because we lack detailed topographical knowledge of this area, it is hard to judge whether this plan would have been practical. The tide was still low in the early morning, leaving the usual fringe of mud flats and marsh along most of the shoreline there. Clinton was an admiral's son, but had no experience with amphibious warfare. (He botched his first effort—an unsuccessful attack on Charleston, South Carolina, in the summer of 1776.) Gage reportedly objected that Clinton might be trapped between Prescott and American reserves before Howe could get enough troops ashore to extricate him.

Clinton then urged an attack at once through Charlestown, bypassing the redoubt and driving westward to seize Bunker's Hill and the Neck. Gage apparently also disliked this. Clinton did not write down Howe's and Burgoyne's opinions. Howe supposedly agreed that the redoubt was isolated and incomplete and should be easy enough to deal with. A letter of Burgoyne's states "My two colleagues and myself . . . have never differed in one jot of military sentiment . . . General Gage, for various reasons, preferred an attack in front, and orders were given to prepare for it."[11]

The final decision was to land at Moulton's Point and move across the open countryside to outflank the redoubt on the north and seize Bunker's Hill and the Neck. Subsequent action would depend on the circumstances existing when this was done. This might require several days so the troops would take blankets and extra rations. It was, on the whole, a reasonable plan: It risked little, and might well result in the capture of Prescott's detachment. Its success would depend on which side could more rapidly develop combat superiority on the peninsula.

The orders went out: "The ten oldest companies of Grenadiers, and the ten oldest companies of light infantry (exclusive of the regiments lately landed), the 5th and 38th Regiments to parade, half after eleven o'clock, with their Arms, Ammunition, Blankets, and provisions ordered to be cooked this morning; they will march by files to the long warf.

"— the 52nd and 43d Regiments, with the remaining companies of Grenadiers and Light Infantry, to parade at the same time, with the same directions, and march to the North Battery. - The 47th and first Battalion of Marines, will also march as above directed to the North Battery, after the rest are embarked, and be ready to embark when ordered. - The rest of the troops will be kept in readiness to march at a moments warning.

"One Subaltern, one Serjeant, one Corporal, one Drummer, and twenty privates, to be left by each Corps for the security of their respective encampments. - Any man who shall quit his rank on any pretence, or shall dare to plunder, or to Pillage, will be executed without mercy.

"The Pioneers of the Army to parade Immediately and March to the South Battery where they will Obey such Orders as they will receive from Lieutt Colo Cleaveland."[12]

The artillery to accompany this force was to consist of four light 6-pounders, four light 12-pounders, and four 5½-inch howitzers, with sufficient artillerymen and attached infantrymen to handle them. The 12-pounders and howitzers must have been clumsy brutes to embark and disembark (possibly it was for this work that the regimental pioneers were put under Cleaveland), but the howitzers' high trajectory made them the best type of artillery for dealing with an entrenched enemy. (See Appendix I) Each gun was to have sixty-six rounds of ammunition. According to Howe, only two howitzers actually were taken.[13]

Howe, being the senior major general, would command the operation on the Charlestown Peninsula. Clinton was assigned the responsibility ". . to remain on the Boston side . . . for the purpose of forwarding reinforcements to General Howe." That done, Gage—as at Ticonderoga and probably at the Monongahela—vanished from the scene. Snug in his headquarters, he gave no more orders, took no apparent interest in the actions of that bloody day. His planning had been grossly incomplete, ignoring a basic principle of the art of war—that a main attack should be preceded or accompanied by a secondary attack, designed to distract the enemy and pin down as many as possible of his troops. An advance—even only a well-simulated one—out across the Boston Neck would have threatened Thomas's unfortified position around Roxbury, and set Ward worrying for his small—but irreplaceable—supplies in Cambridge. It certainly would have made him most reluctant to reinforce Prescott. Gage had the men and guns to spare for such an operation, including his light dragoons who would have been an awesome thing to raw Americans. Intelligently handled, this force would have run no risk. But Percy, commanding the British defenses at Boston Neck, could only contribute ". . a pretty smart cannonade [which] we kept up from there upon Roxbury in order to amuse the Rebels on that side."[14] Gage's nonchalant abdication of his responsibility as commander in chief left Ward free to concentrate against Howe.

Two ancient myths have accompanied this mustering of the British forces. One is that the British soldier was grievously overloaded with ". . an estimated weight of a hundred pounds for each man."[15] In fact, he carried sixty rounds of ammunition, cooked rations for three days, and his blanket. Added to his uniform coat, musket, accouterments, and full canteen, this came to something between forty and fifty pounds—weight enough on a warm day, but lighter than his usual heavy marching order of sixty-odd pounds.[16] His uniform was not appreciably more uncomfortable than the civilian clothing most Americans wore, being cut to much the same pattern, if slightly snugger and smarter. His long leggins had been replaced by comfortable half-gaiters, and many of his officers were more concerned with practicality than appearance.[17]

The other myth insists that the British dawdled in their preparations and finally launched a tardy, slapdash attack because of their contemptuous belief that Americans would never stand up and fight. A good many Englishmen did despise American military qualities, and not without reason. During the French wars the average New England provincial regiment had performed poorly in action and never seemed to take care of itself in camp. General James Wolfe was only a little harsher than many of his fellow officers in his famous stricture of 1758 ". . the dirtiest most contemptible cowardly dogs you can conceive. There is no depending on them in action. They fall down dead in their own dirt and desert by battalions, officers and all."[18] But Howe, Abercrombie, and others had served with competent Americans, and the average Englishman in Boston had sober thoughts of Concord/Lexington

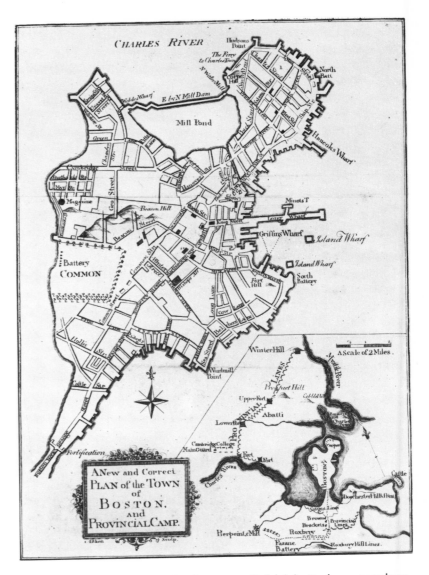

Map of Boston showing wharfs, streets, British batteries, magazines, &c., published about a month after the Battle of Bunker's Hill in the July 1775 issue of Robert Aitken's *The Pennsylvania Magazine or American Monthly Museum*, edited by Thomas Paine. (*American Maps and Map Makers of The Revolution* 2/2.)

and Noddle's Island. Howe's preparations were as careful as his limited means permitted. He took no more liberties with his American opponents than he would have with an equal number of French regulars.

The council ended (apparently around 7:00 AM); the British went hurriedly about their preparations. Rations were cooked and issued, ammunition checked, additional artillery emplaced in the Copp's Hill battery which kept slugging at Prescott's diggers. "These guns were well pointed & struck the redoubt every time, but they still continued their work." Rawdon noticed that "They struck it several times, but being at a great distance, and the work of an extraordinary thickness and solidity, they could make no impression on it."[19]

Howe and Graves went aboard the *Somerset*, intending to have her warped into position off Moulton's Point to cover the landing but the water proved too shallow.[20] Graves therefore transferred large numbers of men from his three big ships to his smaller ones. An officer and thirty-six men went aboard the *Symmetry*, twenty seamen joined the *Falcon*, whose crew had been much reduced by casualties and desertion. (See Chapter III) The *Preston* found the crew and ammunition for the *Spitfire* sloop; other ships did the same for the two gondolas. The ships' bigger boats were armed, equipped, and manned, ready for shifting troops.

The sloops-of-war took up their assigned positions. At 8:00 the *Lively* hauled up its anchor and went about the laborious work of warping down to a new position off Moulton's Point. With its new hands aboard, the *Falcon* moved up to join her. Anchoring at 10:00, its captain put "springs on our cable" to get his broadside to bear on the redoubt and ". . began to fire round shot, grape, and small arms."[21] The *Glasgow* held its original position, firing both at the redoubt and any sign of American movement on the Charlestown Neck. At 11:00 the *Symmetry* joined her. Shortly thereafter her officers ". . saw a Number of Rebells going into Charles Town. fired several Shot at them."

Meanwhile Lieutenant Colonel Thomas James, Royal Artillery, took his two gondolas in as close to the mill dam as he could, and began firing at anything that attempted to cross the Charlestown Neck. Accounts of the gondolas' effectiveness vary. Clinton thought they performed "great service;" an unidentified English officer felt that they didn't ". . get so near as they ought;" and Graves contented himself with noting that neither the *Glasgow*, *Symmetry*, nor the gondolas were able ". . to approach within the distance desired . . ." the tide still being at the ebb during the early morning.[22]

Prescott and his men could only dig, duck when the Copp's Hill 24-pounders went off, and endure. Those that had time to watch could see the increasing stir throughout Boston, the marching redcoats, the purposeful bustle of ships' boats. They had challenged England—and an unknown answer to their challenge was preparing.

CHAPTER IX
UNDER A VERY WARM FIRE

Either late on the 16th or early the next morning, Ward made what he considered sufficient preparations for the relief of Prescott's detachment. General Orders issued at Cambridge on the 17th directed that Nixon's, Little's, and John Mansfield's Massachusetts regiments and 200 Connecticut soldiers ". . with two days provisions and well-equipped with arms and ammunition . . . be on parade at five o'clock [that afternoon] ready to march." Putnam signed the order for the Connecticut detachment, but set the time an hour later.[1] Normal military procedure would have been to relieve Prescott in the *morning* of the 17th, especially if there were any danger that his tired men might be attacked. The fact that this relief was scheduled for the evening suggests that Ward may have believed Prescott to be busy in relative security on Bunker's Hill. If so, the sound of the *Lively's* guns was as much of a surprise to him as it was to Gage.

Subsequent actions of the American forces are difficult to reconstruct. Ward's orders to his troops in the Cambridge-Medford area seem to have been most oral and therefore easily garbled or misunderstood, especially if transmitted by an aide-de-camp or courier who did not fully comprehend their meaning. No American headquarters—including Ward's—kept a proper journal, showing orders received or issued and actions taken, and the time at which these events occurred. Watches were not synchronized (a practice apparently introduced to the American Army by Von Steuben during the winter of 1777-1778 at Valley Forge). Even the best officers had little idea of the necessary details involved in handling an army in action. Through the French wars, English officers like Abercrombie and Bradstreet had seen to planning, orders, and supply, and usually had done it efficiently and quickly.

From Breed's Hill, as the protective darkness faded, Prescott could see how completely isolated his position was. All around his unfinished redoubt, the hill sloped gradually away, with no natural obstacles to prevent it from being outflanked on either the north or south. Americans stationed in Charlestown might protect his southern flank, but to the north there were only open hayfields stretching all the way down to the Mystic River. To partially cover this northern flank, he started men building a breastwork ". . about 20 rods (330 feet) in length from the fort northerly, under a very warm fire from the enemy's artillery."[2]

Exactly what sort of fortification Colonel Gridley intended to construct on Breed's Hill remains unclear. In European practice—exemplified by the defenses constructed around West Point later in the war by expert French military engineers—a redoubt was a simple square fortification, to be defended by infantry alone. Artillery would be emplaced to its flanks or front in separate, lower defensive works so that the two arms could give each other mutual support without getting in one another's way.[3] However, the work on Breed's Hill never was properly finished. It was built during darkness or under fire, by untrained men, according to the plans of an amateur engineer with extremely little practical experience. Moreover, Gridley did not supervise the final states of the work—in Prescott's words ". . the engineer forsook me" about sunrise.[4] Captain Henry Dearborn of Stark's Regiment, who had at least a distant look at these fortifications, recalled that ". . the ramparts had been raised to the heighth of 6 or 7 feet, with a small ditch at their base, but it yet was in a rude or imperfect state." The Reverend Peter Thatcher, writing from information he got from Prescott and others, reported that the completion of the redoubt and breastwork was prevented by the ". . intolerable fire of ye enemy." An unknown soldier remembered ". . the earth which they threw up for a breastwork [was] very dry and loose, for they had only one of these short nights to execute it in."[5] According to a gentleman named William Tudor, "I was in the Intrenchment at 8 Saturday at which time our people had nearly got the Breast Work [he probably meant the rampart of the redoubt] finished, but the Embrasures were not cut, nor the Platform for the Cannon prepared, there were no cannon there, only two field pieces, 4 pounders."[6]

The redoubt and breastwork were roughly built and unfinished, but they did offer protection. The Americans would have to expose only their heads and shoulders when they stood up to fire (". . intrenched up to their chins . . ." in Percy's words). Unless some embrasures were cut after Tudor's departure, Captain Gridley's two 4-pounders could not have fired effectively from inside the redoubt, even if that had been the original intention. (A ridiculous fantasy has developed in recent years that the desperate American gunners blasted out their own embrasures by firing their cannon into the rampart of the redoubt.) There is no clear statement as to where these guns were posted. One British witness said ". . in the corner of the redoubt . . . ," but this still leaves the situation thoroughly vague.

The intensity of the British bombardment also has been variously reported. Prescott had thought it "very warm." Lieutenant Colonel Experience Storrs of Putnam's Regiment who ". . about 10 went down to Gen. Putnam's post who has the command [Putnam then was somewhere on the Charlestown Peninsula] . . ." thought the fire from the ships ". . but moderate . . . Some shot whistled around us. Tarried there a spell . . . one killed and one wounded when I came away."[7] Private Peter Brown and Thomas Boynton were in the redoubt together: Brown thought there was a lull in the firing before 11:00; if Boynton noticed one, he did not record it.

All accounts agree that one of the first shots—probably fired by the *Lively*—killed an American, identified as Private Asa Pollard of Bridge's Regiment, who had been working in the redoubt's ditch; ". . many others escaped very narrowly." The first casualty always is a shock: Men gather, gawk, and feel their stomachs turn over. Prescott ordered Pollard buried immediately, but this disregard of traditional spiritual comforts was another shock to many of his soldiers. One of them identified himself as a clergyman, and Pollard was given as formal a funeral as possible, in defiance of Prescott's orders. Then some of the fainter-hearted began to seep quietly off toward the Neck.

Putnam had ridden out from Cambridge when he heard the *Lively*'s guns. Apparently he conferred with Prescott; at any rate, after looking over the situation, he rode off to Ward's headquarters to secure more men for what promised to develop into a most satisfactory brawl. Much time and energy have been spent attempting to prove that Ward had placed Putnam in charge of operations on the Charlestown Peninsula. The assumption is most doubtful: He had no official authority whatever over either Massachusetts or New Hampshire troops. In fact, throughout the entire battle the Americans were ". . commanded without order, and God knows by whom" as Major General Charles Lee sardonically described their situation. But Putnam, being Israel Putnam, would naturally involve himself in any available action and try to take charge of it.

Prescott had many problems and even more complaints. Putnam, Tudor, and probably other very important persons had been buzzing around him; Colonel Gridley's departure had forced him to be his own engineer. Also, as he remembered it, Colonel Bridge and Lieutenant Colonel Brickett ". . being indisposed, could render me but little service, and most of the men under their command deserted me." (In fact, both officers were wounded during the battle, and their two regiments had some ninety casualties out of approximately 500 men engaged.)

More important, Prescott's detachment still was very much alone. No reinforcements or supplies had reached him, no Americans had appeared on Bunker's Hill to organize a supporting position there. Some of his subordinates urged him to send for fresh troops to relieve them. Prescott refused, declaring (in words undoubtedly bowdlerized for the edification of posterity) that "The works should be defended by those who built them: their honor required it and they could do it successfully."[8]

His soldiers however were increasingly apprehensive and harder to keep at work. Peter Brown, a company clerk in Prescott's own regiment, remembered ". . we Saw our danger, being against Ships of the Line, and all Boston fortified against us. The danger we were in made us think there was treachery, and that we were brought there to be all slain, and I must and will say that there was treachery oversight or presumption in the Conduct of our officers. . . . many of our young Country people [deserted], apprehending the danger in a clearer manner than others who were more deligent in digging & fortifying ourselves. We began to be almost beat out, being fatigued by our Labour, having no Sleep the night before, very little to eat, no drink but rum, but what we hazzarded our lives to get, we grew faint, Thirsty, hungry, and weary."[9]

Many of these new soldiers had neglected to bring the prescribed day's ration with them. Few had canteens, and a lucky British cannon ball smashed the two hogsheads that held their water supply. There was water in plenty in the Charlestown wells, but getting it under fire from the ships and Copp's Hill was risky. These were young farmers and small-town artisans for most part, accustomed to regular hours, full meals, plenty of sleep, and a slow-moving world. Guns pounded at them; every so often someone was hurt. Prescott tried to keep them busy: the interior of the

redoubt was finished off with banquettes, or firing steps.[10] To set an example, Prescott reportedly strolled along the top of the redoubt. But the slopes of Bunker's Hill behind him remained bare; the sun was higher and hotter, and a dust cloud from the digging hung over his sweaty, thirsty men. Around 9:00, Prescott finally told Major John Brooks of Bridge's Regiment to go to Cambridge and ask Ward for reinforcements. Brooks turned to Captain Samuel Gridley in hope of borrowing an artillery horse to speed his journey. Gridley—supposedly citing the risk of that the animal might be killed while crossing the Neck—refused. Brooks trudged off across Bunker's Hill.

The process of reinforcing Prescott meanwhile was getting under way, though slowly and with reluctance. Dashing back to Cambridge, Putnam had found Ward suffering from a bad attack of his "stone." (It is possible that Putnam had to begin by explaining just how Prescott happened to be on Breed's, instead of Bunker's Hill.) From all the grumble of artillery fire to the east, Ward could guess that there would be trouble, soon and in large quantities. Unlike Putnam, he was not going to immediately mount his horse and ride off in all directions: Gage could strike at Charlestown, the Boston Neck, Dorchester, or even across the Back Bay to Lechmere's Point, or up the Charles River. Until he was certain of what Gage would do, Ward would not weaken his center around Cambridge to commit larger forces to the Charlestown Peninsula.

Still, it would be necessary to make certain that Prescott had a fighting chance—should worse come to worst—of withdrawing safely. Ward sent an "express" to Stark, ordering him to send 200 men to Prescott's assistance. Stark got this message about 10:00 and at once sent off his Lieutenant Colonel Isaac Wyman with this detachment. Captain John Callender's Massachusetts artillery company with its two light guns also was ordered to Breed's Hill.[11] And, though nothing is certain, it is likely that other detachments also were dispatched. Detached companies from Little's, Doolittle's, and Benjamin Woodbridge's Massachusetts infantry regiments seem to have taken up positions in Charlestown around noon—quite possibly the "Rebells" reported by the *Glasgow*.

These reinforcements secured, Putnam went galloping back across the Neck, heedless of the warships' fire. Ward turned to a multiplicity of routine responsibilities while he waited to see what Gage would do. Around 10:00 he was again interrupted by the arrival of Major Brooks with Prescott's demand for reinforcements and supplies. (By one account, once across the Neck, Brooks at last had been able to find someone who would trust him with a horse.) He urged Prescott's requests strongly: Ward remained stubborn. We can guess that other officers and influential civilians around the headquarters supported Brooks. At last, rather like a village constable taking a difficult citizen before the local Selectmen, Ward consulted the Committee of Safety.

CHAPTER X
GO AND OPPOSE THEM

At noon, the *Preston*'s signal halyards broke out with the flags, "All boats manned and armed." The *Glasgow* sent her yawl, the *Boyne* her longboat, the other warships and transports the largest boats they had.[1] By 1:00 PM these boats were at the different wharfs and the embarkation under way. The monotonous bombardment from the ships and Copp's Hill dwindled. Americans could watch with grim interest, to see which direction this mustering landing force would go.

In Cambridge the Committee of Safety had paused in considering the shortage of ammunition and similar pressing problems to give attention to Ward's dilemma. Warren, its leader and most incisive mind was absent, down with a sick headache from overwork, though this may not have made any difference in their final decision. About noontime, after much argument, the Committee sided with Major Brooks—Prescott must be reinforced.

At Roxbury Thomas's command was in high excitement. If Gage came out across Boston Neck, Thomas either would have to stand and fight in the open or withdraw. In a tardy attempt to improvise fortifications, he had trees felled across the streets and posted his regiments on the best ground available. Spencer's Connecticut Regiment retired to the summit of a nearby hill—where it remained through the following night. Learned's Massachusetts Regiment marched to its alarm post at ".. the burying ground . . . where we placed an ambush with two field pieces placed to give it to them unawares, should the regulars come."[2] At this hour, there was little else Thomas could do.

The purposeful noise and movement in Boston suddenly paused. Out from the wharves came a precise double column of big boats, bright with scarlet and steel. Graves' junior officers managed this miscellaneous collection of small craft with rare competence. (One of them, Midshipman Cuthbert Collingwood, would be an outstanding admiral through the Napoleonic Wars.) As the boats moved steadily northward there could be no doubt that their objective was the Charlestown Peninsula.[3]

Few battles have been more of a public spectacle. The roofs of Boston were black with civilians, Patriot and Loyalist alike, all with their own prayers and fears. Every hillock on the north bank of the Mystic River and the western side of the Back Bay had its knot of spectators. It was a magnificent show in the clear sunlight, especially when the British warships and the Copp's Hill battery began firing harder than ever. (By English standards, of course, it was a minor affair—nothing compared to Amherst's landing near Louisbourg in 1757, employing over 300 boats and ending with Wolfe's grenadiers, light infantry, Highlanders, and rangers storming ashore through surf and rocks against entrenched French troops.) Off Moulton's Point the *Lively* and *Falcon* now joined by the little *Spitfire*—raked the landing area to flush any lurking Americans. From the Back Bay, the *Glasgow* switched some guns from the Charlestown Neck to ".. annoy the Rebels while troops landed." The *Symmetry* and the two gondolas kept banging at the Neck, where more targets were appearing. (About this time the *Symmetry* ran out of ammunition and had to be resupplied from the *Glasgow*.) Many of the ships' guns lacked the range or elevation to hit the redoubt, but the Copp's Hill 24-pounders hammered its face, and the howitzers and mortar emplaced there did their best to drop shells inside it.

This swelling bombardment finally provoked a reply from Captain Gridley, providing the battle with its one comic opera touch. Peter Brown watched while Gridley ".. fired a few times then swung his Hat three times round to the enemy and ceased to fire." Burgoyne, standing among the busy gun crews on Copp's Hill, noticed only ".. two cannon balls that went a hundred feet over our heads." An unidentified "British officer in Boston" wrote home that ".. they fired seven or eight shot into the North end of the Town; one shot went through an old house, another through a fence and the rest struck the face of Cobb's [sic] hill."[4]

Word of the British movement came to Cambridge in hot haste. Whether or not Ward already had begun issuing orders to reinforce Prescott, his problem now had been solved in part for him. The only question remaining was whether this was Gage's main attack or only a feint. While the Cambridge bells pealed a "General Alarm," and drums crashed out the long, rolling beat that meant "To Arms," Ward began moving troops. Nine Massachusetts regiments, Stark's and Reed's New Hampshire regiments, and at least two more companies of artillery were to march at once.[5] The Massachusetts regiments designated were Jonathan Brewer's, Nixon's, Gerrish's, Doolittle's, Woodbridge's, and James Scammon's, with the remaining men of Frye's, Bridge's and Prescott's. Some companies of Gerrish's which were guarding Chelsea (on the mainland just north of Noddle's Island) were recalled. Captain Israel Putnam Junior (acting as his father's aide-de-camp) came pounding back with orders to bring up his company and that of Captain John Chester from the Connecticut troops.

At the same time, Ward ordered Gardner's Regiment to Prospect Hill to reinforce Patterson's Regiment which was already there. Ward's own regiment was sent to Lechmere's Point, then held by Sargent's four New Hampshire companies. Lieutenant Colonel Storrs of Putnam's Regiment reported for orders; Ward told him to defend "Fort Number One" (See Chapter VI). These regiments gave him a sketchy defensive line across the eastern approaches to Cambridge.

The result was immediate confusion. Ward had no staff to guide and supervise this movement. In several regiments the officers were completely unfamiliar with the local topography and roads; no one seems to have had a map of the area. Ward's orders may have been unclear; their delivery certainly must have been leisurely. Stark, some four miles away in Medford, did not receive his until ".. about 2 o'clock."[6] This was a time of testing, and it quickly proved that Ward's colonels were neither a band of brothers nor of heroes. Captain Dearborn wryly described the result ".. extremely irregular and devoid of everything like concert—each regiment advancing according to the opinions, *feelings* or caprice of its commander."[7] Regiments frayed away as they advanced, unwilling officers and men dribbling from their ranks. These were locally recruited units, friends and neighbors serving together: Captain Joshia Smith and Sergeant Lemuel Brown were hardly more than "Josh" and "Lem" from down the lane—to be humored and obeyed after a fashion during drill and camp routine, but scarcely endowed with absolute authority to march another free New Englander into danger. Consequently, there was reluctance alike to obey and to enforce obedience. Captain John Chester came across one company whose ".. captain had mustered them and ordered them to march and told them he would overtake them directly, but they never saw him till next day . . . the most of the companies in this provience [Massachusetts] are commanded by a most despicable set of officers . . . for almost all from the captain general [Ward] to a corporal are afraid to set up proper martial authority and say, as affairs are situated, they think their people will not bear it . . . ."[8]

There also were last-minute delays: When the New Hampshire troops (this again from Dearborn) were "paraded," Stark discovered that many were short of ammunition. Each man was thereupon issued ".. a gill cup full [four ounces] of powder, fifteen balls, and one flint." This they hurriedly made up into ammunition to fit their individual muskets. Those with bullet molds and cartridge boxes may have made cartridges; most seem to have carried their powder loose in horns, pouches, or even pockets. If the bullets did not fit their muskets, they had to be melted or beaten into slugs of the proper caliber.[9] Then Stark and Reed moved out; it was three miles—a good hour's march—more to Breed's Hill, and the artillery fire was echoing louder as the minutes ticked away.

Howe's first wave—those ten "oldest" companies each of grenadiers and light infantry, the battalion companies of the 5th and 38th Foot—spilled out of their boats at Moulton's Point at 2:00 PM. Oars flashing, the boats backed off and headed again for the Boston wharves. That trip would be harder, pulling against the running tide; close to an hour would be needed to return, embark the second wave—the battalion companies of the 43d and 52d Foot and the artillery—and bring them to Moulton's Point.

Watching from Breed's Hill, Prescott quickly guessed the British plan. Between the northern end of his breastwork and the Mystic River there was an open gap of over 200 yards through which the British could march straight toward Bunker's Hill, completely cutting his communications. By this time, Captain Callender's artillery company may have reached the redoubt.[10] Prescott ordered an artillery officer—probably Captain Gridley—to take two guns and "..go and oppose them." Captain Knowlton with his Connecticut detachment was to support the guns. The two units marched off, and Prescott lost sight of them. It would seem that he wanted the artillery to advance toward Moulton's Point and fire on the British waiting there, or at least to occupy a blocking position across the slough from the northern end of his breastwork. When the guns and Knowlton did not appear there, he concluded they had retired to Bunker's Hill. As far as the artillery was concerned, he was correct: Putnam met the company retreating down the western slope of Bunker's Hill ".. in great haste; he ordered the officer to stop and go back; [the officer] replied that he had no cartridges; the General dismounted and examined his boxes, and found a considerable number of cartridges, upon which he ordered him back; he refused until the General threatened him with immediate death; upon which he returned to the hill again, but soon deserted his post, and left the cannon. Another officer ... conducted much in the same manner."[11] Whatever the sordid details, Prescott ended up with two light fieldpieces, but no artillerymen to man them.

Captain Thomas Knowlton, however, was living up to the reputation for intelligent daring he had established in the French Wars before he was seventeen. Over six feet tall, lean and sinewy, a natural leader, he would meet an untimely death at Harlem Heights fifteen months later, leading his picked rangers in a successful counterattack.[12] On this day he calmly assessed his chances: His force was too small for offensive action, the artillery had run away, but Prescott's left (north) flank must be covered. The best position he could find was approximately 600 feet to the left rear of the breastwork where a ".. fence half of stone and two rayles of wood ..." ran north from the slough to the Mystic River. "Here nature had formed something of a breastwork or else there had been a ditch many years agone." Knowlton's men stacked arms and went to work tearing down a nearby parallel rail fence, and then rebuilding it just in front of their position. Part of the meadows in this area having been mowed and the hay left on the ground to dry, they packed the loose hay tightly between the two fences. Howe would describe this improvised fortification as ".. a breastwork made with strong railing taken from the fences and stuffed with Hay, which effectively secured those behind it from Musquettry."[13] Here Knowlton was joined by Lieutenant Colonel Wyman with the 200 New Hampshiremen from Stark's Regiment. (Prescott's version was that around 2:30 PM ".. a party of Hampshire, in conjunction with some other forces ... lined a fence at the distance of three score rods back of the fort, partly to the north.")

Shortly thereafter Prescott sent ".. Lieut-Col. Robinson and Major Woods, each with a detachment, to flank the enemy."[14]

He did not know where they went, or what they did thereafter, but ".. had reason to think ... they behaved with prudence and courage." Their departure left him, so he asserted, with ".. perhaps one hundred and fifty men in the fort," a figure that is hard to believe and certainly does not take into account the men defending the length of the breastwork, or holed up in Charlestown. Peter Brown's version was ".. about 700 of us left, not Deserted, besides 500, reinforcement that could not get nigh enough to us to do us any good till they Saw that we must all be cut off ... then they ventured to advance." Certainly there had been considerable desertion from Prescott's detachment—the odd aspect of it being that there is no mention of any effort by Prescott and his subordinates to check it.[15]

In fact, the American forces on the Charlestown Peninsula were steadily building up. A considerable force was collecting on Bunker's Hill, though part of it must have been men who had deserted Prescott. Charlestown also was held in some strength—the Committee of Safety's official report placed it at ".. one or two regiments ..." (adding the brazen claim that these had been withdrawn before the action began).[16] Other units were coming forward, often by companies and detachments so that no coherent listing is possible. It appears that five out of the nine Massachusetts regiments designated by Ward were on the peninsula (at least in part) by 3:00 PM.

Stark and Reed reached the Neck to find *Glasgow*, *Symmetry*, and the two gondolas raking it with their fire—in probable cold fact firing a gun or two every few minutes. Round shot ricocheted lazily across the narrow strip of land, dismantling shot screeched weirdly overhead. In the last bit of cover west of the Neck, two milling regiments blocked the road, unwilling to go forward into the fire. Colossal Major Andrew McClary—six-foot-six of rawhide frontier veteran—strode forward through the muttering soldiers to tower genially above their white-faced colonels. Colonel John Stark's compliments, and—if Massachusetts didn't happen to need the road just then—would they mind moving over to let New Hampshire through? Massachusetts quickly scrambled into the ditches along the road (doubtlessly with duly opprobrious remarks); New Hampshire got more-or-less in step again and went tramping out onto the Neck. With a two-regiment target passing before them, the British gunners stepped up their fire. Stark kept to the normal rate of march, ignoring them completely. Dearborn, captain of Stark's leading company, suggested that ".. quickening the march of the regiment ..." might be wise. Stark's reaction obviously made Dearborn hunch his shoulders when he wrote about it, forty-four years later. "With a look peculiar to himself, he fixed his eyes on me and observed with great composure—'Dearborn, one fresh man in action is worth ten fatigued men'." New Hampshire marched across the Neck and up Bunker's Hill. Not a man, it seems, was even slightly nicked.[17] Behind them, at least part of Massachusetts found heart to follow.

The naval bombardment of the Neck continued, but there is little evidence it caused many casualties. The range was too great, the guns and gunners not good enough. On Breed's Hill knowledge that the warships were attempting to cut off reinforcements created some extra uneasiness; Peter Brown picked up a rumor that ".. one cannon cut three Men in two on the neck." It well may have happened—or some soldier in one of the units which crossed the Neck under fire may have thought that Prescott's people needed taking down a couple of pegs. However, the ships' fire was spectacular enough to frighten any American willing to be frightened. Many Americans considered it excuse enough not to cross the Neck, and to that extent the naval gunfire was effective.

Howe came ashore with the second wave of his force. Sending four companies of light infantry forward along the bank of the Mystic River to a covered position some 400 yards east of the Rail Fence, to screen his movements, he formed the rest of his 1,550 infantry in three lines on Moulton's Hill—a tight formation, ready to deploy in any direction. The artillery, gotten ashore by main strength and awkwardness, was put into position on the forward slope in front of them. At 3:00 PM it opened fire. While Howe studied the American positions, his men were told to sit down and eat their noon meal.

At this time legend again enters the story. "Just before the action began, Gen. Putnam came to the redoubt, and told Col. Prescott that the entrenching tools [used to construct the redoubt] must be sent off, or they would be lost; the Colonel replied, that if he sent any of the men away with the tools, not one of them would return: to this the General answered, they shall every man return. A large party was then sent off with the tools, and not one of them returned; in this instance the Colonel was the best judge of human nature."[18] The story is from General Heath's memoirs—but Heath was in Roxbury all day, and there is no firm eyewitness confirmation of his tale.

Certainly it was essential to get the entrenching tools back to Bunker's Hill if any reserve position were to be constructed there. It would have been simple common sense for Putnam to have sent men forward to get them, and this may have been what he actually did. Surgeon Thomas Kittredge of Frye's Regiment took some wounded men from the redoubt to the rear about this time; later he recalled that he saw Putnam on the west side of Bunker's Hill and ". . heard General Putnam request some of the men to go up to the fort and see if they could get some of the entrenching tools."[19]

One way or another, Putnam got his tools, but his troubles were only beginning. Someone laid out a defensive work on the crest of Bunker's Hill, but it was difficult to get men busy digging. For one thing, these were Massachusetts troops and he was a Connecticut officer. For another, those men he did put to work didn't move much dirt. Bunker's Hill provided a wonderful view of the action—and officers and men were far more interested in watching than working.

CHAPTER XI
IF HE WISHED THE PLACE BURNED

From Moulton's Point Howe examined the American lines through his telescope. It was going to be a rougher affair than it had seemed from Boston in the early morning.

"On the first view, it was clearly seen that the rebels were in force and strongly entrenched upon their right, in the Redoubt that had been seen from the town at daybreak; with cannon, and with a large body of troops posted in the houses of Charles Town about 200 yards distant from the right [south] of the Redoubt. Their left and center were covered by a breastwork (part of it cannon proof) which reached from the Redoubt to the Mystick, the space from the Redoubt to that river being about 380 yards, and the whole extent they occupied about 600 yards . . ."[1] There was a large force of Americans visible on the crest of Bunker's Hill, and—even as he looked—a column came swiftly down the face of the hill to reinforce the American left flank.

Howe sent back to Boston for reinforcements—the 47th Foot, the 1st Battalion of Marines, and the remaining companies of grenadiers and light infantry which had been waiting at the North Battery for just such a contingency. He also dispatched orders for the two gondolas to work their way around the peninsula into the Mystic River and enfilade the American left flank. In theory, such small gunboats could move either by oars or sails, and could take advantage of breezes too light to move larger ships. These, however (See Chapter III), were unable to work against the tide; they may have gotten into the Mystic River at the very end of the battle, but too late to be of any use. Clinton thought they should have been left in their original station.[2]

The terrain before Howe was deceptively open: Hayfields studded with small clumps of trees stretched up the slopes of Breed's and Bunker's hills. The tops of several brick kilns showed in the low ground to the right of Breed's. Because of Gage's and Montresor's negligence, Howe could know no more of this seemingly gentle landscape's hidden obstacles than if he had just landed in North Africa. Under that hay—grown almost waist-high in places—was typical New England pasture land—rocky and uneven, and cut by the slough which extended from the kilns westward into the depression between Breed's and Bunker's hills. Worse, there were ". . . ten or twelve rows . . ." of stout-built fences ". . . formed of strong posts and close railing, very high, and which could not be broken readily . . ." which would repeatedly check the British advance.[3]

The shortage of boats had prevented the transport of any horses for the senior officers and artillery. Had Howe or some of his aides been able to ride forward to examine the ground and inspect the American lines at close range, they would have detected the weak section of the American defenses—the unfortified 200-yard, east-west gap between the north end of Prescott's breastwork and the south end of the Rail Fence. Probably they would have seen how weak and thinly spread Wyman's and Knowlton's detachments were along the Rail Fence. Certainly they would have been able to select the easiest lines of advance for their artillery. Such reconnaissance would have been safe enough because of the inaccuracy of the 18th century musket; a mounted officer 100 yards from the American lines would have been hit only by accident.

While Howe waited, his men munched their rations, watching their artillery bombard the redoubt and breastwork. Lieutenant Rawdon felt it was ammunition wasted ". . . it was so strong that our balls had no effect upon it, and their men kept so close behind it that they were in no danger."

The column which Howe saw coming down Bunker's Hill was Stark's and Reed's regiments. They had reached the crest of the hill to find Putnam trying to introduce some order among a considerable number of Americans who had stalled there. By some stories, Putnam wanted to detain all or part of the New Hampshiremen to work on his fortifications. If so, he was brushed aside. Stark caught the situation in mid-stride: The British were preparing to attack; the American left flank was very weak. Pausing only long enough to let the tail of his column close up, he gave his men a few words—politely described as ". . short, but animated . . ."—and took them downhill at the double to the Rail Fence. Senior by rank, experience, and character, he took charge of its defense. His first step was to continue the fortifications to the water's edge. The Rail Fence had ended at the cut bank (". . 8 or 9 feet perpendicular height . . .") of the Mystic River. Below this was a beach, rather narrow now at high tide. Stark had his men build a wall of stones taken from nearby fences across it. Then he ". . set a mark eight or ten rods [roughly 50 yards] distance . . ." to the front of this position, ordering his men not to fire until the enemy passed it.[4] The Rail Fence would offer little protection against artillery fire, but the force holding it was cohesive and tough, led by experienced officers. Knowlton's

Connecticut detachment was the only "foreign" element there, but Knowlton was a veteran of the same hard service. Also, this force—unlike Prescott's which was divided among Charlestown, the redoubt, and the breastwork—was all in one line, enabling Stark to keep them under his eye and control.

At some point during the afternoon the continuing movement of British troops to the Charlestown Peninsula convinced Ward that this must be the only British attack. He therefore fed in (in what hour and sequence we do not know) Little's, Whitcomb's, Mansfield's, and Gardner's regiments, almost stripping Cambridge's defenses. Around 4:00 PM he released his own regiment (led by its Major Edward Barnes) and Sargent's New Hampshire companies. The major result was to increase the existing confusion, mightily assisted by a report from Colonel Sargent that "A large schooner with from five to six hundred men . . ." was attempting to gain a landing near Lechmere's Point. Probably Sargent had seen the *Symmetry* trying to get into position to fire on the Neck, and had imagined the rest. British sources contain no confirmation whatever of any such attempted landing.[5]

The immediate victim of Sargent's bogy was Colonel James Scammon, who was court-martialed after the battle for ". . disobedience to orders and backwardness in the execution of his duty . . ."—his accusers being several of his lieutenants. Scammon supposedly had marched "about noon," none too certain as to which road to follow. Shortly afterwards he met "expresses" who said that the British were landing at Lechmere's Point. As he conceived a good soldier should, Scammon headed for the Point; on arrival he found "General" John Whitcomb already there, seemingly with Colonel Asa Whitcomb's Regiment. What John Whitcomb was doing there is not exactly clear, but Ward probably had sent him in response to Sargent's alarm. He did rank Scammon. Scammon claimed that Whitcomb ordered him to go to a "small hill" near by and keep an eye on the British "floating batteries." At the court-martial Whitcomb denied giving any such orders; he had told Scammon to ". . go to the hill," meaning Bunker's Hill. Four of Scammon's officers backed their colonel's word. Whatever the truth, Scammon marched away again, took post on a small rise approximately a mile west of Bunker's Hill, and sent two sergeants forward to hunt up someone in authority and find out ". . if his regiment was wanted."[6]

Major Scarborough Gridley did not choose to cross the Neck as ordered. Instead, he took position on a hill to the west of it and made a show of engaging the *Glasgow* with his little 3-pounders. The *Glasgow* never realized that it was under attack; at least there is no such entry in either of its logs.

Along with the reinforcements trickling into Charlestown Peninsula came two generals, Warren and Pomeroy. Like Whitcomb, they had not yet been formally commissioned, but their authority as such was commonly accepted. However, both chose to come as "volunteers"—in other words, to waive their rank and to fight practically as privates. Both were popular figures and commanding personalities: In an army desperately short of effective generals, their action further crippled Ward's ability to control his forces.

The old stories relate that Warren met Putnam on Bunker's Hill and that Putnam offered to turn over his command to him. (Again, there is this unsolved question of whether Ward had placed Putnam in command of the American forces on the Charlestown Peninsula, or whether Putnam simply had taken over on his own hook.) Warren refused, and asked to be directed to the point where the fighting would be the hottest. Putnam indicated the redoubt; there, Prescott also offered Warren the command, and again Warren refused it. We do know that Warren—who once had said he would like to die

fighting—was dressed as if for his own wedding. Englishmen who buried him remembered ". . . his fine silk-fringed waistcoat."[7]

Pomeroy had been at home in Northampton on leave. By tradition, Putnam wrote him of the Council of War's decision to ". . draw our forces nearer the city and to take possession of the heights of Charlestown." Pomeroy left Northampton around noon on 16 June and rode through the day and the following night, carrying the musket he had made thirty years before for the first Louisbourg expedition. Reaching the Neck in the early afternoon, he sent his horse back—he had borrowed it and so should not expose it to the warships' fire. He then joined Stark's line along the Rail Fence. Stark did not offer him the command there.[8]

By now the American line had taken on its final form. On the right (south) flank there were one or two regiments—or, more likely, companies from several Massachusetts regiments—in and around Charlestown. Seemingly no one officer was in command here; the troops were scattered by companies through the buildings and fence lines along the town's eastern edge. They may have built some light barricades, since one British officer reported that the line ". . was also prolonged on the right of the redoubt by defenses similar to those improvised on the left."[9]

Next came the redoubt, also held by Massachusetts troops. Prescott commanded here: His own account is not too clear as to whether he also controlled the troops along the adjoining breastwork, but it may be assumed that he did. Colonel Bridge and Colonel Frye were with him.

The empty space between the ends of the breastwork and the Rail Fence was filling up. Some unremembered soldiers had partially plugged it by building three small *fleches* ("V"-shaped defenses, with their point to the enemy), probably of fence rails. Americans stationed here could fire into the left flank of British troops attacking the Rail Fence; conversely, Americans at the Rail Fence could rake the right flank of an attack on the *fleches*. In addition to the *fleches*, there were the fences and trees along an east-west road through this area to provide additional cover.[10] The American forces here never have been identified: Probably they were mostly from Nixon's, Jonathan Brewer's, and Doolittle's regiments.

Then came the Rail Fence, prolonged by the stone wall on the beach, held by the two New Hampshire Regiments and Knowlton's Connecticut detachment. Callender's artillery company reportedly was near the south end of the Rail Fence for a period, and even may have fired a few futile rounds in the direction of Moulton's Point. Soon thereafter he found his ammunition too large for the caliber of his fieldpieces; after an attempt at breaking open the cartridges and loading with loose powder, he and his men abandoned their guns and left the field.[11] Colonel Richard Gridley apparently worked them with improvised crews of infantrymen until he was wounded. However, Captain Samuel Trevett saved the Massachusetts artillery's honor. Crossing the Neck under fire, he brought his two guns up to the Rail Fence and fought them with stubbornness and skill.

Back on Bunker's Hill Putnam raged amid a clutter of stragglers, deserters, malingerers, and disorganized regiments. Contemporary accounts have him all over the American position during the battle, but the consensus is that he remained near Bunker's Hill most of the time, attempting to get the fortifications there finished and to push reinforcements forward. The only regimental commander mentioned as being with him was Colonel Samuel Gerrish, described as ". . unwieldy from excessive corpulence." Putnam obviously did his best to coordinate the efforts of the American forces, but lacked the personal authority and professional skill to carry it through. For all his rough-and-ready energy and popularity, the task was too big for the old provincial ranger.

The number of Americans on the Charlestown Peninsula is as hazy as their command system. The Committee of Safety insisted there were only ". . about 1,500 men, which were the most that were at any time engaged on the American side." Putnam supposedly said 2,200; Stark that there were "2,500 with Prescott alone."[12] More recent historians put the total at from 2,500 to 4,000 though a few somewhat overzealous writers still insist that there were no more than 700 Americans holding the whole front, from Charlestown to the Mystic River. But Ward had piled in his entire left flank and most of his center—roughly 7,000 men and eight guns—in a plain attempt to crush Howe. The British—who, after all, had an excellent chance to count the Americans as they came forward over Bunker's Hill—placed the number at between 4,000 and 5,000.[13] The one certain fact is that Howe was about to attack a fortified position defended by a force considerably stronger than his own.

Over on Moulton's Hill the red mass of troops stirred. The awaited reinforcements were coming into the shore further south between Moulton's Point and Charlestown.[14] Howe organized his force—now approximately 2,200 rank and file—into two divisions; he would lead the right one against the Rail Fence; tiny, gallant Brigadier General Robert Pigot (Howe referred to him as ". . the little man . . .") would take the left against the redoubt. As their divisions deployed into line, the Americans in Charlestown began sniping at Pigot's leading units. It was long-range shooting, but the tight redcoat formations were good targets.

Retribution was quick, and rather overwhelming. Admiral Graves had joined Howe ashore ". . for the sake of seeing whether any further aid could be given, and of ordering it immediately; & whilst he was there the General observing the mischief his left wing sustained by the fire from Charles Town, the Admiral asked him if he wished to have the place burned, and being answered *Yes*, he immediately sent to the Ships to fire red hot Balls (which had been prepared with that in View) and also to Copse Hill Battery to desire they would throw Carcasses, into the town, and thereby it was instantly set on fire in many places . . ."[15] Burgoyne (who was watching from Copp's Hill) wrote that Howe ". . sent us word by a boat, and desired us to set fire to the town; we threw a parcel of shells and the whole was instantly in flames." Other accounts say that naval landing parties also went ashore and set fires along the waterfront. According to ships' logs, the town was well on fire by 4:00 PM. Burgoyne thought it quite a spectacle.[16]

CHAPTER XII
A MOMENT THAT I NEVER FELT BEFORE

William Howe was a somewhat inarticulate man, not given to detailed explanation or smooth descriptions. Ward left no written orders; Putnam no written statement. Burgoyne and Clinton could describe only portions of the action. Gage had no apparent interest in it. Prescott's account is limited to the redoubt, and full of ambiguities. Stark's bare-bone report dismissed the fighting with ". . Accordingly we proceeded, and the battle soon came on." For all its thousands of bystanders and witnesses, much of this battle remains unexplained. The one certain thing is that the common story—three successive British frontal attacks, launched in pomp, pride, and vainglory against the entire American front—is false.[1]

Confronted by what seemed an unbroken American front, Howe had little choice. The afternoon was running out. If he did not clear the Americans from the Charlestown Peninsula before dark, they would be too strongly entrenched by the next morning to even think of attacking them. The gondolas were late; none of the warships could move up the Mystic until there was a favorable wind and time to sound the channel. However, the American left (north) flank—along that odd construction of fence rails and hay—appeared to be still in the process of getting itself organized, and should be the weakest portion of their defenses.

Howe put eleven companies of light infantry into column along the Mystic River beach where they could advance unseen by Americans on the slopes to the south. Their orders were ". . to force the left point of the rebels breastwork [the Rail Fence];" and then to take them in flank. (Stark's stone wall across the beach was equally hidden from Howe by irregularities in the shore line.) The Grenadiers were directed to attack the left of the American line, supported by the battalion companies of the 5th and 52d regiments.[2] Their attack would have to be pushed hard, both to divert Stark's attention from the light infantry's enveloping movement and to exploit its hoped-for success. The artillery's four light 6-pounders, escorted by the grenadier company of the 35th Foot, would go forward with Howe's division to smash up the Rail Fence, opening the way for the grenadiers' bayonets. Successfully executed, Howe's attack would roll up the American line from north to south, cutting in behind the redoubt.

Howe's report did not give his orders to Pigot in any detail, but the latter's obvious mission was to advance deliberately so as to fix the Americans in the redoubt and along the breastwork until Howe's enveloping attack developed.

From Moulton's Hill the 12-pounders and howitzers kept up their bombardment of the American lines, eventually shifting much of their fire to the area of the *fleches*—either against Americans moving into that area or units attempting to advance down the saddle from Bunker's Hill to Breed's Hill. This, combined with the continuing fire from Copp's Hill, would establish a second gauntlet that reinforcements and supplies for Prescott must run.[3] The supporting warships continued their bombardment as long as they could annoy the Americans without endangering their own troops.

Some time after 3:00 PM the British advanced. (Howe may not have waited for all of the 47th Foot and 1st Battalion of Marines to get ashore since they would form Pigot's second line.) He himself went in on foot at the head of his grenadiers: He always had led in person and he would do it now, probably half out of habit, half to set an example to his young soldiers. His staff—twelve officers, including one each from the Navy, engineers, marines, and artillery—marched with him. Unfortunately for the British, in thus playing the part of a battalion commander Howe gave up control of his attack. Pigot would have to fight his own battle; Howe would see only the action immediately around him, with little idea of what his second line and his artillery were doing.

With almost a half-mile to go, the advance was slow because of rough ground and the fences. There were frequent halts to ". . give time for the artillery [probably the accompanying 6-pounders] to fire," and to maintain alignment. To the watching Americans it seemed to take forever.

Peter Brown in the redoubt recalled "The enemy landed, fronted before us, and formed themselves in an oblong square, in order to surround, which they did in part—after they were well formed they advanced towards us in order to swallow us up . . . tho we could do nothing with our small arms as yet for distance, and had but two Cannon, and no gunner, and they from Boston, and from the Shipping firing and throwing Bombs, keeping us down, till they had almost surrounded us . . ."[4]

Most of the American infantry originally seems to have been formed in the usual three ranks behind their defenses, each rank to fire in turn on order and then drop back to reload so that a steady fire could be maintained. (A single rank could not load and shoot fast enough to check a determined attack.) This system usually broke down after a few minutes, and men began firing independently, but by that time the momentum of the enemy attack should have been broken. This enabled the more competent American commanders to exercise a certain degree of fire control. The first round fired by each rank—having been carefully loaded before the action began—would be the most accurate. Subsequent rounds, loaded in haste by jostling, hurried soldiers, might not carry so true. Therefore it was essential that the Americans hold their fire until the British were within effective range—but not so near that their survivors could break in with the bayonet before the second rank could fire. There is the old legend that the Americans were told "Don't fire until you can see the whites of their eyes"— which, a little experimentation will show, would be too close for comfort. It is certain that the Americans were told to wait for the order to fire, to aim low, to pick off the British officers. Apparently Stark set some definite range at which the troops along the Rail Fence were to open fire. That meant waiting until the British were less than a hundred yards away—and that waiting would be desperately hard for many raw, nervous Americans as those glinting rows of British bayonets came steadily nearer.[5] Veteran American commanders had the uneasy foreknowledge that their excited soldiers could blaze away their thirty rounds in no time at all—and that very few of them had bayonets.

The British artillery soon had trouble. Loaded with equipment, straining in their rope harness, shoving against the gun carriages, twisting at the gun wheels, the crews could not keep up with the grenadiers. Every fence was a delay. Possibly looking for easier ground, they seem to have strayed off to their left, where they bogged in the northern edge of the slough. Lacking gun horses, the 6-pounders had to be tugged and grunted out by manpower while the attack went on without them. As usual, the infantry was going to get the dirty end of the stick.[6]

Down on the narrow beach of the Mystic River the light infantry's snake-like column-of-fours moved swiftly ahead. How far they were from Stark's stone wall when they first saw it is not clear, but they attacked immediately. At fifty-odd yards range, Stark gave the order: his first volley almost wiped out the light company of the 23d Foot, the "Royal Welch Fusiliers" who led the column. Through the smoke, across the tumbled fusiliers, thrust the light infantry of the 4th Foot, "the King's Own." Stark's second volley smashed them down. Over that welter charged the light company of the 10th Foot, to be shattered when Stark's third rank fired. Caught between cutbank and river, unable to deploy, the light infantry fell back, carrying their wounded. Behind them ninety-six dead huddled on the narrow beach—". . as thick as sheep in a fold" was one American's incongruous thought.

Across the meadows above the beach Howe came on. His first line was his ten companies of grenadiers in company columns, his second the battalion companies of the 5th and 52d. Approximately ninety yards from the Rail Fence the grenadiers deployed from column into line; Dearborn, waiting with poised musket near the south end of the fence, remembered the parade-ground ". . precision and firmness . ." of the movement, and that the grenadiers then opened fire by platoons.[7] Howe's version was that "Their orders were executed by the Grenadiers and 2 battalions with a laudable perseverance, but not with the greatest share of discipline, for as soon as the Order [formation] with which they set forward to Attack with

Bayonets was checked by a difficulty they met in getting over some very high fences of strong railing under a heavy fire, well kept up by the Rebels, they began firing, and by crowding fell into disorder, and in this state the 2d Line mixt with them—the Light Infantry at this same time being repulsed, there was *a Moment that I never felt before*."[8]

Some of Knowlton's Connecticut detachment apparently had fired prematurely. A Lieutenant Dana explained it with what must have been considerable mendacity: He had fired, so he declared ". . with a view to draw the enemy's fire, and he obtained his end fully, without any damage to our party."[9] What he meant was that his nerve broke, and he fired before Knowlton gave the order. This would have touched off firing by his immediate command, spreading on down the line as other Americans thought the order had been given. Caught crossing a fence, the British began to fire back instead of continuing their advance, as troops usually do when their attack meets a check. The second line jammed into the grenadiers but, between the fences and the Americans' fire, could not restore the attack's momentum. Had the pioneers—whose function was to open gaps in just such obstacles as that fence— been with the grenadiers instead of Colonel Cleaveland, the attack might have been made with considerably more effect.[10]

As it was, after a few minutes of useless fire-fight the British sagged sullenly back out of effective range, leaving a windrow of dead and broken comrades. Some excited Americans jumped the fence and started out in pursuit; officers quickly corralled them before the British could catch them in the open and drive them back upon the Rail Fence, masking their comrades' fire. The veteran officers went along the lines, praising, correcting, and reorganizing. They had served with British soldiers in the old wars, and knew this first clash had been only a short grace before dinner.

Pigot had advanced with the battalion companies of the 38th, 43d, and 47th regiments, the 1st Battalion of Marines, and three companies each of grenadiers and light infantry. Their exact formation at this time is not certain. They seem to have come forward in line, firing by platoons once they got within long range, to fix Prescott's attention ". . a feeble attack . . . at long shot." Prescott's reaction was that the British ". . fired very hotly at the fort, and meeting with a warm reception, there was very smart firing on both sides." The British seemingly suffered few casualties; the Americans almost none, but Prescott had allowed his men to fire away irreplaceable ammunition.[11]

Quickly regrouping his forces, Howe formed a new plan. Once more we only can deduce its details: Howe knew now that the beach was a trap, but he seemingly realized that the lightly fortified east-west sector between the breastwork and the Rail Fence was the weak link in the American defense, despite its three *fleches* and the patches of slough in front of it. A breakthrough there would outflank both the redoubt and the Rail Fence; a general attack all along the front would keep the Americans pinned down while this was accomplished. It would be rough work but with close artillery support it should succeed.

Howe brought his light infantry in on his right to attack the Rail Fence. The grenadiers and the battalion companies of the 5th and 52d would storm the *fleche* area. Pigot would carry the breastwork and the redoubt. In less than a half-hour the British advanced again.

For Howe's division it was disaster, endured to the limits of human courage. "As we approached, an incessant stream of fire poured from the rebel lines; it seemed a continued sheet of fire for near thirty minutes. Our Light-infantry were served up in Companies against the grass fence, without being able to penetrate— indeed, how could we penetrate? Most of our Grenadiers and

Light-infantry, the moment of presenting themselves lost three-fourths, and many nine-tenths, of their men. Some had only eight and nine men a company left, some only three, four, and five."[12] Again the British artillery support failed; Trevett's cannon raked them at short range.[13] Stopped dead, the redcoats hung on desperately in the open, shooting at the American defenses as fast as they could load. It only increased their losses; behind cover, the Americans rested their muskets on the fence rails to fire with surer aim, officers and men firing together. They made special efforts to pick off the officers, conspicuous for their bright scarlet coats and gorgets as well as their courage—two or three Americans might aim at the same man to make certain of him. Most of the British bullets went high over their heads.[14] Finally, it was more than even British infantry could stand. The survivors stumbled back, Howe walking with the last of them. Most of his staff had been shot down around him; his uniform was splattered with their blood.

Pigot advanced on the breastwork and redoubt. A capable commander, he combined his direct assault with an effort to envelop the redoubt on its left (south) by a drive between it and still-blazing Charlestown. This last mission probably was given the battalion companies of the 47th Regiment and the 1st Marine Battalion though there is some question that all of these units were involved. (See Chapter XIII) Inside the redoubt, Prescott's men braced themselves. They had been sifted through a day of duty, a night of labor, and most of another day of toil, hunger, danger, and thirst. Cowards and weaklings had slunk away; the men remaining were of the old New England rock. Prescott had realized that his ammunition was running low. "I commanded a cessation [of firing] till the enemy advanced within thirty yards, when we gave them such a hot fire that they were obliged to retire nearly one hundred and fifty yards before they could rally . . ." To watchers in Boston it was ". . a continual sheet of Lightening, and an uninterrupted peal of Thunder" and ". . an incessant stream of fire . . ." On Pigot's left, his enveloping force ran into a hornets' nest—Americans driven from Charlestown had set up a strong center of resistance around a stone barn and its outbuildings to the southwest of the redoubt. Scattered Americans were firing from cover all around the town. Pigot's attack staggered, fired back fruitlessly for some minutes like Howe's had done and then retired, possibly on orders.[15]

A few panicked Englishmen may have fled toward the landings, to be driven back by officers with drawn swords, but most of them once more rallied just out of effective range. Howe was demanding why his artillery had again failed him—the answer came that most of the solid-shot ammunition the 6-pounders' crews had so laboriously carried along in their advance had turned out to be for 12-pounder guns. They did, however, have the proper caliber of grapeshot, and Howe told them to use it.[16] The range was rather long for grape to be effective, but at least it would keep the Americans' heads down. Meanwhile, somebody had better hustle some 6-pounder solid shot forward.

The fault for this ammunition failure was Cleaveland's. His neglect of duty (See Chapter V) already was a bitter jest, and this capped it. It is possible that some of the attached infantrymen—only partially trained and possibly not too bright—may have picked up the wrong boxes of ammunition; if so, the artillery officers present were not doing their duty. Cleaveland's excuse managed to misrepresent every fact of the case: He had sent sixty-six ". . Rounds to each gun, not more than half was fired . . . The men sent on purpose to Carry the Boxes of Ammunition after the Cannon went a Plundering and occasioned it to be said that one of the Guns wanted ammunition. A commanding officer of Artillery

cannot be in every place." Cleaveland had remained in Boston; what he really was doing there during the battle does not appear. If Admiral Graves could come ashore to see that the most effective naval support possible was provided, it does seem that Colonel Cleaveland should have been where his guns were in action.[17]

Howe had one eye on Bunker's Hill where the number of Americans was steadily increasing. Small detachments were continually trickling forward, most of them to the Rail Fence. Probably British officers picked up indications that the hill was being fortified. For all Howe could know, the Americans on Bunker's Hill were as good soldiers as those now opposing him. If they got well dug in along that commanding ridge, they would be impossible to dislodge. If he failed to maintain the initiative, they might counterattack. Howe sent to Clinton for further reinforcements and shifted his troops for another attack. The Copp's Hill battery resumed its hammering at the redoubt. It was echoed from the Back Bay where *Glasgow* and *Symmetry* still interdicted the Neck. By now, it was something after 4:00 PM.

CHAPTER XIII
TO GET AT THE LIVING

England was far away. Howe left off being a colonel of grenadiers and became a general. One more unsuccessful attack would cripple Gage's army so badly that it might not be able to hold Boston; to retreat was to invite an overwhelming counterattack, with the same ending. Some of the officers around him, wild with shame and anger, were for another headlong attack; others urged that the risk and probable loss were too great. We can only guess his thoughts: Possibly there was an echo of his old commander, James Wolfe. "In war something must be allowed to chance and fortune, seeing that it is in its nature hazardous, and an option of difficulties; that the greatness of an object should come under consideration, opposed to the impediments that lie in the way; that the honor of one's country is to have some weight . . ."[1]

While the squadron's boats pulled in to pick up the wounded carried down to them, the artillery hustled for ammunition, and reinforcements mustered on the Boston wharves, Howe considered his problem. For a start, several companies of the 47th Foot and 1st Marine Battalion cleared his left flank, flushing American snipers from the northern edge of Charlestown and silencing that troublesome strongpoint around the stone barn.[2]

Clinton and Burgoyne had watched the battle from Copp's Hill. The sight of Pigot's repulse—Burgoyne said Pigot's division was "staggered," Clinton claimed he saw it ". . give totally way . . ."—made Clinton boil over. Receiving Howe's request for more reinforcements, he paused long enough to order the 63d Foot and the 2d Marine Battalion to ". . embark and follow . . ." and to ask Burgoyne ". . to save me harmless to General Gage for going without his orders." Then, commandeering a warship's small boat, he had himself ferried over to the Charlestown Peninsula. "I landed under fire from the town: two men were wounded in the boat before I left it. I wrote to General Gage, informing him of the critical state of matters. I then collected the guards and such wounded men as would follow—which, to their honor, were many—and advanced in column with as much parade as possible to impose on the enemy."[3]

The American line was loud with pride and rejoicing—which dampened as the shattered redcoat regiments formed up again and the British guns reopened fire. Men checked powder horns and cartridge boxes and found them almost empty. Prescott discovered

SITUATION MAP #1 opposite: First Attack, c. 3:30 P.M.
(1) Rail Fence: Stark, with his and Reed's New Hampshire regiments and Knowlton's Connecticut detachment. (2) *Fleches*: Identity of original force unknown. Probably reinforced by part of Prescott's regiment. (3) Breastwork: Troops from Frye's, Bridge's and Prescott's Massachusetts regiments, apparently under Prescott's command. (4) Redoubt: Troops from Frye's, Bridge's and Prescott's regiments commanded by Prescott; also Samuel Gridley's Massachusetts artillery company. (5) Charlestown: Held by men from Prescott's regiment and apparently companies from Little's, Doolittle's and Woodbridge's Massachusetts regiments. (6) Elements of Brewer's, Nixon's and Doolittle's Massachusetts regiments, moving into *fleche* area. (7) Bunker's Hill: Putnam, with Gerrish's Massachusetts regiment and other troops. (8) British light infantry, of Howe's division, attacking along the beach of the Mystic River. (9) British grenadiers, of Howe's division, attacking Rail Fence. (10) 5th and 52d Foot, of Howe's division, following the grenadiers. (11) 38th and 43d Foot, of Pigot's division, making a holding attack on breastwork and redoubt. (12) Three companies each, grenadiers and light infantry, Pigot's division, in holding attack. (13) 1st Marines and 47th Foot landing to join Pigot. (A) Moulton's Hill: Battery of 12-pounders and howitzers. (B) 6-pounders bogged down. (C) General position: *Lively, Falcon, Spitfire.* (D) Original position: Gondolas. (E) General position: *Glasgow* and *Symmetry.* (F) Direction: Copp's Hill battery. (G) Stone Barn.

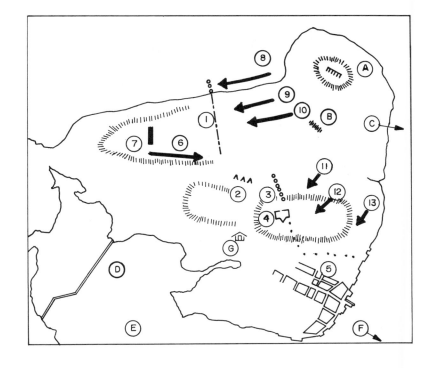

SITUATION MAP #2 opposite: Second Attack, c. 4:00 P.M.
(1) Rail Fence: No change. (2) *Fleches*: Elements of Brewer's, Nixon's, Doolittle's and Prescott's regiments. (3) Breastwork: No change. (4) Redoubt: Infantry units, no change. Artillerymen have deserted. (5) Charlestown: On fire, forcing most Americans to withdraw, many taking up positions on the northern and western edges of town and around stone barn. (7) Bunker's Hill: Putnam with Gerrish's regiment, stragglers and deserters from front line. (8) Light Infantry attacking Rail Fence. (9 & 10) Grenadiers and 5th and 52d Foot attacking *fleche* sector. (11 & 12) 38th, 43d Foot and companies of grenadiers and light infantry attacking breastwork and redoubt. (13) 1st Marines and 47th Foot attempting to envelop redoubt. (A) Moulton's Hill: Battery of 12-pounders and howitzers. (B) Approximate position: 6-pounders, out of proper ammunition. (C) General position: *Lively, Falcon, Spitfire.* (D) Gondolas moving toward Mystic River. (E) General position: *Glasgow* and *Symmetry.* (F) Direction: Copp's Hill battery. (G) Stone barn: Converted to American strong point. (H) Trevett's Massachusetts artillery company.

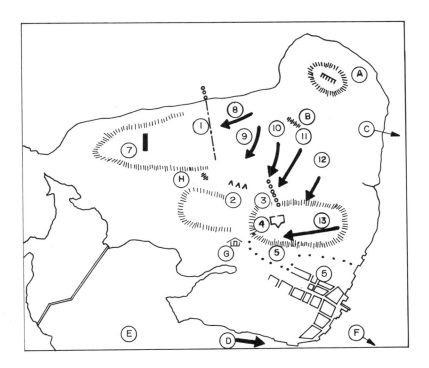

SITUATION MAP #3 opposite: Third Attack, c. 4:30 P.M.
(1) Rail Fence: Reinforced by a few volunteers from Gerrish's and other regiments. (2) *Fleches*: No appreciable change. (3) Breastwork: No change. (4) Redoubt: No change. (5) Charlestown: Americans driven from stone barn area; some still in Charlestown. (6) Elements of Gardner's and Little's Massachusetts regiments, three Connecticut companies and other troops. (7) Bunker's Hill: No appreciable change. (8) Light Infantry skirmishing with Stark's command. (9) 52d Foot attacking *fleche* sector. (10) Grenadiers and 5th Foot attacking breastwork. (11) 38th and 43d Foot attacking redoubt. (12) Companies of grenadiers and light infantry attacking redoubt. (13) 1st Marines and 47th Foot enveloping redoubt, with elements pursuing some American troops driven from stone barn. (14) 2d Marines and 63d Foot landing. (A) Moulton's Hill: Battery of 12-pounders and howitzers. (B) 6-pounders enfilading breastwork. (C) General position: *Lively, Falcon, Spitfire.* (D) Gondolas in Mystic River. (E) General position: *Glasgow* and *Symmetry.* (F) Direction: Copp's Hill battery. (H) Trevett's remaining gun in action.

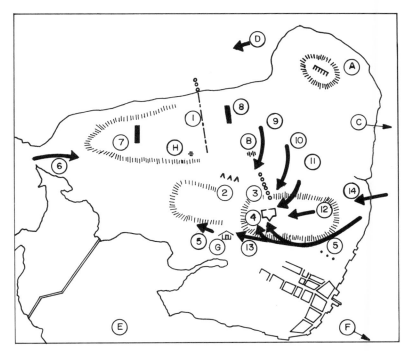

33

".. Our ammunition ... nearly exhausted ...";
at the Rail Fence, Dearborn had run out of ammunition and was scavenging for more among the dead and wounded. Prescott broke open the cartridges left with the two abandoned fieldpieces and shared out the coarse gunpowder they contained. In the redoubt and along the breastwork there was time for men to feel the grindings of hunger and thirst as they counted their remaining rounds. The British were between them and the Charlestown wells. Neither food, drink, nor ammunition had come forward from the rear. But, under Prescott's eye, they would endure.

In Cambridge, Ward also waited, ignoring the pain of his sickness. He had done his best to overwhelm Howe, putting in almost every man and gun he had in his center and his left. If Gage suddenly were to sally out across the Boston Neck, he would have no reserves to send to Thomas's support. Cambridge itself was guarded only by Patterson's Regiment and elements of two Connecticut regiments. Now, the battle's outcome was up to his colonels and to Putnam. Ward also had ordered supplies sent forward. (The Boston Public Library has an order, signed by his secretary Joseph Ward, directing that two barrels of something to be sent to ".. the Troops at Charlestown.")[4] Getting such supplies to them would be the problem. Even if teamsters could be found willing to risk the passage of the Neck, there still would be the increasingly dangerous trip forward from Bunker's Hill to the redoubt. Anything potable or edible that did get across the Neck undoubtedly was consumed by the crowd of reluctant heroes lingering on Bunker's Hill.

Between Cambridge and the Neck, Ward's colonels still were at their marching and countermarchings. Even the most willing were slow. Deserters, stragglers, fugitives, sightseers, and stray details clogged the roads. Chester's Connecticut company had been alerted ".. just after dinner ..."; it had marched promptly (only taking time to cover their conspicuous blue-and-red uniforms with ".. our frocks and trousers ...", to avoid attracting an undue share of British attention), but would not reach the battlefield until around 4:30. Three other regiments marched at the same time, but by the time Chester reached Bunker's Hill ".. there was not a company with us in any kind of order."[5] Little's, Gardner's, Whitcomb's, Mansfield's, and Ward's regiments—or at least considerable parts of them—had not yet reached the Neck. Mansfield never did: He halted somewhere west of it, and would be cashiered ".. For remisness and Backwardness in the execution of his duty." Scammon sat on his chosen little hill ".. three quarters of an hour, during all which time there was a smart fire on Bunker's Hill ..." and impatient junior officers gnawed their knuckles and muttered Biblically phrased reflections on their colonel's ancestry.[6]

On Bunker's Hill there was increasing chaos as more units came panting across the Neck and stalled there, staring out across the battle. Most of these Americans, from drummers to colonels, never had heard a shot fired in anger before this day. Unlike Prescott's men, they had not had hours of gradual toughening, to learn that it took a lot of long-range artillery fire to kill one man. Still untrained and half-disciplined, they had been hurried across the Neck where ".. the cannonshot ... buzzed around us like hail ..." and into a roaring, all-out fight.

An occasional cannon ball from the *Symmetry* or *Glasgow* went skimming and bounding across the hill's lower slopes; further out, explosive shells from Copp's Hill burst thunderously around the redoubt. Wounded men dribbled back from the front lines, and there were dead men sprawled on Bunker's Hill itself. The British infantry had fired high in their assaults on the Rail Fence; most of their bullets had passed harmlessly over the heads of the Americans there and struck the rise of Bunker's Hill behind them. Sometimes—quite by accident—their blind dropping killed or wounded men who had thought themselves safe. A few years more, and many of these same Americans would face British fire unflinchingly, closing their ranks as their comrades fell. Now, officers and men together, they broke ranks to seek shelter ".. behind rocks and hay-cocks, and thirty men, perhaps, behind a single apple tree." They were assiduous in helping the wounded: ".. twenty ... were glad of an opportunity to carry him away when not more than three could take hold of him to advantage."

If Putnam ever had exercised any real control of the situation, he lost it now. He ordered, coaxed and cursed, but officers and men would neither dig nor advance. He whacked some of the most cowardly with his sword, but it put no courage into the rest. Fat Colonel Gerrish may have tried to help him, or may have found a safe spot and reported himself completely exhausted—both stories were told later by reputed eyewitnesses. Occasionally a junior officer, such as Adjutant Christian Febiger of Gerrish's Regiment, was able to collect a group of the better soldiers and take them forward.[7] Most of these went to the Rail Fence or the *fleches* which were nearest Bunker's Hill. Few, if any, reached Prescott.

Suddenly, the brief lull was over.[8] Once more Howe had swiftly changed his troop dispositions to match a new plan. On his right flank, the survivors of his eleven companies of light infantry, approximately 150-200 strong, shook out in skirmish formation opposite the Rail Fence. Dearborn saw them ".. only a few small detached parties ... which kept up a distant, ineffectual, scattering fire." Their mission was double: to fix Stark's command, and to cover the flank of the 6-pounders. Supplied with ammunition of the correct caliber, the 6-pounders were trundled into a position from which they could enfilade the length of the breastwork. The artillery officers must have pushed their guns well forward, close to the north edge of the slough, because twelve artillerymen were wounded.[9] Possibly some of the 12-pounders were dragged up from Moulton's Hill to join them.

The grenadiers and the battalion companies of the 52d and 5th regiments were deployed in a single line. (While awaiting the order to advance, they may have done some long-range volleying at the American lines.) Apparently the 5th was to attack through the *fleche* area, the grenadiers and the 52d against the northern end of the breastwork.

Pigot would storm the southern end of the breastwork and the redoubt, the 38th and 43d regiments' battalion companies on his right, his light infantry and grenadiers in his center; on his left the battalion companies of the 47th Foot and the 1st Marine Battalion would swing wide around the redoubt to storm it from the west and get into its rear. This attack would employ the greatest part of Howe's troops to pinch out the redoubt. That taken, they would be astride the saddle between Breed's Hill and Bunker's Hill, in the best possible position either to continue the advance against Bunker's Hill or to meet a counterattack from the Americans there.[10]

There were bandaged, limping officers and men in these regiments. A shocking proportion of their officers were gone, sprawled somewhere in the trampled, blood-flecked grass. Senior enlisted men took their places: In the light company of the 35th Foot the new commander was a private, with four more to follow him. Major Pitcairn of the Marines had two wounds but would not quit his men. Someone ordered the troops to drop their haversacks and rolled blankets; soldiers threw off their coats. England was far away, but they were Englishmen. Duke's son, poacher's bastard, and guttersnipe's brat—Howe gave the word, the drums crashed out, and they swept forward.

It was quick and brutal. Firing as fast as their sweating crews could sponge and load, the British 6-pounders scourged the whole length of the breastwork. Some of the Americans there fled into the redoubt; others broke for the rear. The units holding the *fleche* area were battered savagely; the best of the American officers were hit as they recklessly exposed themselves, attempting to halt the disintegration of their line. Colonel Frye and Colonel Nixon were wounded. In Jonathan Brewer's Regiment, Colonel Brewer, Lieutenant Colonel Buckmaster, and Adjutant Butler all were down. Major Willard Moore, who had led Doolittle's Regiment into action, was badly hurt; as his men tried to carry him to the rear, he was hit again and would die of it. Near the south end of the Rail Fence, Captain Trevett still had one gun going but his other one was out of action.[11]

Stark's men could only watch. At best, if they held their position a few minutes more, they might be able to cover Prescott's retreat. If they lingered too long, the British might cut in behind their right (south) flank and pin them against the Mystic River. Amateur military historians have criticized Stark for not counterattacking to envelop the British right (north) flank. Had such a move been sensible, Stark probably would have attempted it. But— though he outnumbered the light infantry in front of him—his men were almost out of ammunition. Very few had bayonets. Their ability to maneuver in the open under fire was questionable; there were no dependable reserves to support him. To attack would mean an advance across those same fence lines that had checked the British so drastically; behind them would be a row of British fieldpieces, belching grapeshot, supported by vengeful light infantrymen—altogether, a good way to get killed uselessly.

At the redoubt Prescott had his men hoard their remaining ammunition, giving the order to fire when the British were a mere twenty yards away. The effect was devastating, but only for seconds. The British piled into the ditch and up against the outer slope of the rampart—any man on either side who popped his head up was likely to get it shot off. Lieutenant Rawdon thought the Americans held with uncommon courage and stubbornness. Rawdon's unit, the grenadier company of the 5th Foot, must have struck the sally port between the south end of the breastwork and the redoubt: His company commander, Captain Harris, recalled that they attacked a ".. breach in their fortifications ..." Even as they reached the ditch, Harris took a scalp wound. Over his objections, Rawdon ordered four soldiers to carry him to the rear. Such a compact target drew American fire; three of the soldiers were wounded, one mortally, but they got Harris to safety. Another bullet went through Rawdon's cap.

By now the British were across the breastwork, though some units possibly were halted by a cross fire from the redoubt and the *fleches*. On the other flank the 1st Marine Battalion, followed by the 47th, worked across broken ground to the south and west faces of the redoubt. Adjutant John Waller of the Marines reported: ".. So we closed upon them; but when we came immediately under the work, we were checked by the severe fire of the enemy, but did not retreat one inch. We were now in confusion, after being broke several times in getting over the rails, etc. I did all I could to form the two companies on our right, which at last I effected, losing many of them while it was performing. Major Pitcairne was killed close by me, with a captain and a subaltern, also a sergeant and many of the privates: and had we stopped there much longer, the enemy would have picked us all off. I saw this, and begged Colonel Nesbitt of the 47th, to form on our left, in order that we might advance with our bayonets to the parapet. I ran from right to left, and stopped our men from firing; while this was doing, and when we

had got in tolerable order, we rushed on, leaped the ditch, and climbed the parapet, under a most sore and heavy fire ... [12]

"Nothing could be more shocking than the carnage that followed the storming of this work. We tumbled over the dead to get at the living, who were crowding out of the gorge of the redoubt."[13] Waller thought that the Marines and the 47th were the first into the works. There was one tight-drawn split-second as the first British officers to get on top of the rampart were shot down—Waller noted ".. three captains of the 52d ..." Then, instantly, the redcoats poured over it, bayonets stabbing. With the redoubt almost surrounded, Prescott ordered a retreat. Most of his men headed for the open gorge at the back of the redoubt, Prescott and some diehards covering the rear with swords and clubbed muskets. A few Americans were throwing rocks but the bayonets were everywhere. Dust and powder smoke made it so dim inside the redoubt that one American had to ".. feel about for the outlet."[14] Peter Brown stayed ".. in the fort when the enemy came in, Jump'd over the walls and ran half a Mile, where balls flew like hailstones and Cannon roard like Thunder ..." Stepping long, with his sword up, Prescott somehow got off unhurt, though bayonets ripped his coat and waistcoat. Colonel Bridge took a sword cut across his face and neck. The seriously wounded were left underfoot, Bridge's Lieutenant Colonel Moses Parker among them. Afterward, an English officer counted thirty Americans "killed by the bayonet" inside the redoubt.

These Americans had one moment of grace as the British untangled their converging attacks. Then the British began to fire: their volleys smashed at the fugitives. Almost at once Joseph Warren dropped with a bullet through his head.[15] It all had happened in minutes: The battalion companies of the 2d Marine Battalion and the 63d Foot were still landing; Clinton's raggle-taggle little column had not yet caught up with the attack. But in front of Howe loomed Bunker's Hill, its crest dark with more Americans.

CHAPTER XIV
A POOR STONE FENCE

From burning Charlestown to the Mystic, the British pushed forward, infantry reforming into some sort of orderly front, artillerymen panting as they hooked onto their guns and followed. The Americans along the Rail Fence held briefly—their fire seems to have stopped the British attempt to swing in behind Prescott from the north. Then, their own right flank left in the air, their ammunition almost gone, they retreated (said Dearborn who was there) ".. with rapidity and disorder towards Bunker's Hill; carrying off as many of the wounded as possible." They also saved Trevett's one serviceable gun after a hard tussle with eager redcoats. Old Pomeroy went with them—walking backwards, so the stories say, carrying his musket which a British bullet had broken off at the stock.

Bunker's Hill was a madhouse. The fortifications there were not even half-finished, but they could offer an anchor for a determined stand. Americans already on the hill outnumbered Howe's remaining force; more Americans were coming hot-foot across the Neck to reinforce them. But many of the Americans on Bunker's Hill had stayed there because they had been afraid to go down into the battle. Now the battle was coming swiftly to them, and it looked even more unsettling than it had at long range.

Clinton reached the redoubt shortly after its capture. He was shocked, or later professed to have been shocked, by the disorder he found there. (A cipher notation in his manuscripts supposedly translates as ". . . All was in Confusion. Officers told me that they could not command their men and I never saw so great a want of order.")[1] Howe, so Clinton declared, ". . told me that I had saved him, for his left was gone."[2] Seeing that Howe's "left"—Pigot's division—had just captured the redoubt, and that Pigot already was driving for Bunker's Hill, we can doubt that Howe said any such thing; certainly he did not include anything like it in his report. However, Howe had lost his entire staff—two of them killed, ten wounded—and undoubtedly was himself thoroughly wearied: Clinton was fresh and eager and could be useful. "I desired that I might go forward with the light troops, but he might rest assured I should not go further than I found he chose to sustain me. He called me back, I thought a little forcibly, but gave words expressive of the service I had done." Thereafter Clinton, so he remembered ". . ordered [Lieutenant Colonel John] Gunning to remain in the redoubt with 100 [men] with positive orders to keep it, and took with me all the rest." Firmly held, the redoubt would give the British a rallying point if they were driven back from Bunker's Hill.

More Americans were coming, shoving through the flotsam of a losing fight, and there were good men among them. Captain Chester wrote ". . Others were retreating, seemingly without any excuse, and some said they had left the fort with leave of the officers, because they had been all night and day on fatigue, without sleep, victuals, or drink; and some said they had no officers to lead them, which indeed seemed to be the case. At last I met with a considerable company who were going off rank and file. I called to the officer that led them and asked why he retreated? He made me no answer. I halted my men, and told him if he went on it should be at his peril. He still seemed regardless of me. I then ordered my men to make ready. They immediately cocked, and declared that if I ordered would fire. Upon that [the company] stopped short, and tried to excuse themselves; but I would not tarry to hear him, but ordered him forward, and he complied."

What regiments came forward at this desperate moment is uncertain; where they formed is mostly guesswork. There were Colonel Thomas Gardner and Colonel Moses Little, with several Connecticut companies—Chester's and those of James Clark and William Coit. From Chester's brief phrase, ". . we joined our army on the right of the center," it would seem that they came over the southern end of Bunker's Hill and advanced towards Breed's, to cover Prescott's fleeing men. Gardner apparently was the first: He was mortally wounded a few minutes later, and his regiment may not have been completely deployed.[3] Major Michael Jackson of his regiment took over, and was joined by the Connecticut companies ". . just by a poor stone fence, two or three feet high, and very thin, so that the bullets came through." Then, or slightly later, Little also advanced.

Pigot's three companies of light infantry plowed into them for a ding-dong, stand-up fight. The Americans undoubtedly had the edge in numbers; they were mostly fresh troops with full cartridge pouches. They shot straight ". . and very briskly; the regulars fell in great plenty, but to do them justice, they kept a grand front and stood their ground nobly."[4] (Waller noted that the light infantry ". . suffered exceedingly in the pursuit.") The British also shot straight and fast; training, discipline, and regimental pride held them firm. Other units pressed up to support them. Major Jackson was wounded, and ". . we lost our regularity, as every company had done before us . . . every man loading and firing as best he could . . . we fought standing about six minutes." To Lieutenant Joseph Hodgkins of Little's Regiment, with two bullet holes in his coat, that "six minutes" seemed more like ". . about two ours." The Americans held long enough to protect Pres-

cott's retreat; once his survivors had stumbled past them, their officers took them back to the next fence line. Rawdon said it was a running fight thereafter, across Bunker's Hill and down to the Neck; Burgoyne that ". . the retreat was no flight: it was even covered with bravery and military skill." This was the sharpest fight of the day—fighting in the open, for which the British had been trained. ". . Mr. Little, of Turky Hill . . . narrowly escaped with his life, as two men were killed one on each side of him, & he came into camp all bespattered with blood." Captain Nathaniel Warner of Little's Regiment had seventeen men killed or wounded out of twenty-three in action.[5]

Behind these fighting men someone thought they heard Colonel Gerrish bellowing, "Retreat! retreat! or you'l all be cutt off." First, in trickles, then in a flood of panicking individuals, the Americans on Bunker's Hill went from there, crowding, shoving down the back slope toward the Neck, Cambridge, and safety. Colonel Scammon finally had put his regiment on the road to Bunker's Hill. There ". . the shot flew very thick . . ."; the regiment was caught in the rush of retreating troops and pretty well swept away. Some lieutenants claimed Scammon ordered a retreat; other officers weren't certain who started the cry. A few of the bravest pushed on ahead, the rest ran.[6]

Sargent took his four New Hampshire companies forward far enough to get himself wounded. Colonel Asa Whitcomb seemingly was not seriously engaged, having only one officer casualty—possibly his and Mansfield's were the two ". . regiments of our men who were looking on at a distance, but were affraid to advance, [Little] set them an example, it seems, which they did not chuse to follow."[7] Major Edward Barnes, acting in command of Ward's regiment, was charged by one of his captains of ". . haulting his men on their march when ordered to proceed immediately to assist at the engagement on Bunkers Hill, . . . Ordering his men to retreat before he got in Sight of the Enemy . . . [and] . . deserting his men & making his Escape thro his own troops off of Bunkers hill & leaving them without any command."[8]

Putnam stayed on Bunker's Hill as long as there was hope of rallying men to hold it. Fugitives crowded past him, ignoring his appeals to stand and fight. At last he rode off, carrying a ". . number of spades and pickaxes . . ."—probably the only entrenching tools saved that day.[9] Clinton had expected a stand on the crest but there was none. As the peninsula narrowed abruptly to the Neck, the American retreat jammed up in increasing disorder. *Glasgow*'s and *Symmetry*'s powder-grimed gun crews blasted at the helpless mass.

This was Gage's opportunity—the Americans were on the run. Boats, troops, and guns waited for his orders. Feed a fresh brigade in behind Howe to keep up the momentum of his advance—thrust a strong sortie out across Boston Neck, to be the other jaw of a pincers closing on Cambridge and Roxbury—hit, and hit hard!

Gage did nothing.

Howe halted his pursuit on the western slope of Bunker's Hill. Clinton was wild to continue, but Howe would not consent. He might be battle-weary, but he still could count noses and know that he lacked the necessary troops to exploit his costly success. Almost half of his original force had been killed or wounded; the men with him ". . were so much harrassed, and there were so many officers lost . . ." that he could not expect them to do more. His only fresh troops were the battalion companies of the 63d Foot and the 2d Marine Battalion (approximately 600 rank-and-file) which had marched as fast as possible after landing, but had not been able to catch up with the action. These were not enough for an effective pursuit west of the Neck and—with Clinton now playing field soldier on Bunker's Hill—there was no way of getting more reinforcements out of Boston in a hurry. The British set up roughly fortified posts to command the Neck and the north end of the mill dam, and started securing the battlefield. By both American and British sources, it was 5:00 PM.

Defeat did not shake Artemas Ward. Once it was certain that the Americans were withdrawing, he sent Lieutenant Colonel Storrs off with the rest of the Connecticut troops to cover their retreat. Since ". . the regulars did not come off from [advance further than] Bunker's Hill . . .", Putnam put them to fortifying Winter Hill, west of the Neck: ". . we immediately went to entrenching; flung up by morning an entrenchment about 100 feet square. Done principally by our regiment under Putnam's directions, had but little sleep that night."[10] Ward may have raised his voice later that evening when Prescott—sore-nosed over what he considered a callous lack of support—offered to ". . re-take the Heights that night or perish in the attempt, if the Commander-in-chief would give him three regiments with bayonets and sufficient ammunition." Ward's answer was emphatically negative.[11]

For a half-hour or so there was considerable random shooting. Some Americans had rallied among the houses just west of the Neck, and were sniping at the British outposts. The British brought up a 12-pounder and threw a few solid shot into the houses. This largely silenced the American sharpshooting, though some outpost bickering went on all night. About 11:00 PM it apparently built up; the *Glasgow* roused and fired several ". . Broad sides at the Neck to prevent the Rebells Rallying on the Troops."

Another problem was the scattering of Americans who had been cut off by the British advance before they could reach the Neck. Some of them must have hidden out for several days. Howe's orderly book shows that on 19 June all guards and sentries were cautioned to arrest persons ". . of Suspicious Appearance." Some tried to break out. Among the incidents of the mopping up was the killing of Lieutenant John Dutton of the 38th Foot. Dutton suffered much from gout; at the day's end, he had gone a little ways from his unit to change his stockings when his orderly warned him that two armed Americans were approaching. Dutton thought they merely wanted to surrender. Instead, they killed both Dutton and the orderly—and were immediately shot down by some light infantrymen.[12]

Between Charlestown and Boston the squadrons' boats passed and repassed with loads of wounded. It was a painful task, finding men among the trampled grass and the fence corners where they had crept, then carrying them down to the boats. The *Somerset* put six puncheons (80-gallon casks) of water ashore for the troops. In Boston the Loyalists turned out with every available vehicle to help move the wounded to the hospitals, then to whatever buildings could be used to shelter them after the hospitals could hold no more. ". . The streets were filled with the wounded and the dying." Officers and privates alike might have wives and children to lament them or to sit in stunned silence. When Major Pitcairn was brought back dying, Gage sent a surgeon to him. Pitcairn told the surgeon to go take care of men who had a chance of living. His marines mourned that they had lost a father: Burgoyne penned a eulogy for him, and wrote influential friends to urge that some provision be made for Pitcairn's family.[13] Lieutenant Colonel Abercrombie had led the grenadiers, to be wounded in Howe's second attack; he would be dead in a week, but he asked grace for his old forest companion, Israel Putnam—should Putnam be captured—as too brave a man to hang.

Westward from Charlestown Neck there was the confused eddying of scattered regiments. The darkling roads streamed with hurrying men and clumps of men, worn out, shaken, and uncertain. Some would keep on going, heading for some blessed place safe from 9-pounder broadsides and inexorable lines of bayonets. But Winter Hill echoed a dull thudding as the Connecticut men dug their new redoubt. Drums rolled Assembly where the grimmer officers gathered their men for another battle. Slowly dying Colonel Gardner sent his son, who had helped to carry him, back to his regiment. Most of New Hampshire was formed up again, waiting for what might come. To learn what that might be, giant Major Andrew McClary turned ranger once again and went skulking back to Bunker's Hill to lie in the long shadows, watch, and listen. Finally convinced that the British would advance no farther, he started back across the Neck, walking openly once he was out of musket range. A last blind broadside from an English warship killed him.

CHAPTER XV
BUT WANT OFFICERS

There would come a time when Americans would hope to sell the British another hill, at the same price. John Stark could write the New Hampshire Provincial Congress on 19 June that his regiment and Reed's were still in good spirits, convinced that the British had lost three to their one—but their regiments had fought as units and undoubtedly had inflicted heavier casualties on the British than any two other American regiments engaged. Nevertheless, on the 18th Ward's army knew it had been defeated. Some of them had fought well, even heroically. They had seen the backs of the King's grenadiers. But the British had won; and their own army was disorganized and contemptuously mistrustful of many of its officers.

It had been a battle of chance and accident between two raw armies. There can be no doubt that Ward, the careful amateur, had been far superior to the inert Gage as a commander in chief. But Ward had no subordinates with the battle craft and tenacity of William Howe. On the American side it had been a colonels' battle, and too many of Ward's colonels had failed its testing. If Ward had chosen well in sending Prescott to establish the first American position on the Charlestown Peninsula, it was mere good fortune that brought Stark to the Rail Fence in the nick of time. As for the individual soldiers, the best Americans could not match the redcoats' disciplined doggedness, though the luck of the fighting had favored them—the unfavorable breezes that had limited the maneuverability of Graves' warships, the strange failure of the British artillery. Had Howe's guns performed effectively, his first attack might have swept the field; his second one certainly would have.

It also had been a savage battle and a notable killing. In perhaps an hour-and-a-half, in an area something under a half-mile square, at least 1,500 Americans and Englishmen had been killed or wounded.[1] This included almost half of the British engaged.

The initial British report gave 19 officers and 207 enlisted men killed, 70 officers and 738 enlisted men wounded, for a total of 1,034 casualties. [2] This was generally accurate, though it would not include some lightly wounded men who stayed with their units. Also, a good many of the wounded sooner or later died in the overcrowded hospitals. British surgeons noted that many of the wounds were unusually dangerous: Because of their shortage of ammunition—and, doubtlessly, individual cussedness—some Americans had used scrap metal for musket balls.[3] Officer casualties were very high: The British officers had set their men an example of bravery, and had been—as Adjutant Waller put it—". . particularly aimed at." Equally serious were the terrible casualties—in some companies, over eighty per cent—of the picked grenadiers and light infantry. Let it be remembered that there have been few times in history when soldiers have taken such punishment and come on again to win.

American casualties are much harder to establish. Ward's order book showed 115 killed, 305 wounded, 30 captured. These figures normally are accepted as the total American loss, but may cover only the Massachusetts troops. Stark wrote the New Hampshire Congress that his and Reed's regiments together had a total of 19 killed and missing and 74 wounded. Information on Connecticut casualties is sketchy, but they appear to have been relatively light. In all, American losses probably can be given with no greater accuracy than somewhere between 400 and 600: Ward's army never was very good at getting its paper work straight or on time, and right now it was in a high state of confusion.[4] The Americans also abandoned five fieldpieces and several hundred hard-to-replace entrenching tools.

In one category American losses were far heavier than those of the British. An unknown—but considerable—number of Americans simply went home after the battle. Stark's report ended by urging that the New Hampshire Committee of Safety "..immediately recommend to the several Towns and Parishes . . . the necessity of stopping and sending back all the soldiers . . . they may find there from the Army, not having a furlough from the commanding officer." It took time to get such faint-hearts back to their regiments, but the New England local governments cooperated wholeheartedly. Gage's spies told him ".. any man that returns home without a pass is immediately seized and sent back to his Regiment."[5] In the meantime, however, their absence left Ward's regiments dangerously weak.

All of the thirty Americans captured seem to have been wounded, most of them seriously. Even with the best of medical attention some of them would have died. But they were to be the first victims of the British Army's two most vicious camp followers—Joshua Loring and William Cunningham, respectively the Boston sheriff and the army provost marshal.[6] Loring was a refugee Loyalist of excellent family; Cunningham a glib Irish adventurer. Both were corrupt and brutal; both robbed and starved their charges far beyond the routine mistreatment normal to 18th century prisoner-of-war hospitals. Before Burgoyne and others learned of their plight, twenty of the thirty were dead of abuse and neglect.

The major British casualty of Bunker's Hill was the plan to occupy Dorchester Heights. This had been scheduled for 18 June, and Clinton urged that it be carried through while the Americans still were in disorder. It should have been quickly successful. On the 18th, to cover the work details fortifying Bunker's Hill, Howe sallied out across Charlestown Neck and burned the houses at its western end where American snipers again were active. His artillery fired on every party of Americans that appeared within range, and he kept his outposts well forward.[7] Though there were rumors that Gage was about to attack across the Boston Neck, Ward nevertheless thought it necessary to detach 1,000 Massachusetts and Connecticut troops from Thomas to reinforce his left flank, now reorganizing between Winter's Hill and Prospect Hill.[8] Thus weakened, it is unlikely that Thomas would have made any effort to dispute a British landing on the Dorchester Peninsula, particularly if it had been combined with an advance—or even the threat of one—across the Boston Neck directly against Roxbury. Except for a few outposts, there were no Americans on Dorchester Heights.

Once more, Gage would not move. Clinton continued his nagging; Graves probably supported him. Giving in, Gage set the operation for the 24th, though it could have gone sooner. The three gondolas were ordered around from the Mystic River where they had been covering Howe's right flank. To beef up the assault force, the 2d Marine Battalion and the 63d Foot were brought back from the Charlestown Peninsula, and the flank companies of the 64th Foot ordered in from their peaceful garrisoning of Castle William. For the first time a combined operation seems to have been set up, either by Gage or through agreed cooperation among his subordinates. Howe was to at least threaten an advance across Charlestown Neck, and the batteries at Boston Neck would bombard Roxbury with incendiary shells, while the landing force went in along Dorchester Peninsula closely supported by gondolas and light warships.

As before, too many people talked. Over on Bunker's Hill Lieutenant Barker's diary entry for 22 June included "..the three Gondolas went away; something suspected to be going on." On the 23d he noted ".. great talk of some expedition tomorrow .." and listed the troop movements. Early on the 24th the landing force embarked; Howe had "All the Troops on this side . . . drawn out and paraded on [Bunker's] Hill, and some marched into the road [across the Neck]." Then Gage called the operation off.

Barker heard that it was because the Americans ".. had got intelligence and had reinforced that place with 4,000 Men." Lieutenant Williams said it was because ".. signals were observed from several places made by the Rebels ..", giving the impression that they had occupied the Dorchester area in force during the night. Major Kemble gave the headquarters' version: ".. the Enemy appearing to have taken the alarm, and our numbers not very strong . . . it was thought proper to lay the project aside, especially as our Guns from the Block House were thought to be sufficient to dislodge them should they attempt to annoy us from thence."[9]

Seeing how ineffective the Copp's Hill battery had been against Prescott's redoubt, Kemble's reliance on the Block House battery to clear Dorchester Heights comes off as a silly piece of face-saving. Ward does seem to have learned of Gage's plan, and to have shifted some troops to support Thomas. But Thomas had neither occupied nor fortified Dorchester Heights; had he wanted to oppose the British landing, he would have had to come out of his improvised Roxbury defenses and fight in the open. The real reason for calling off the attack was Gage's instinctive abhorrence for even the most carefully calculated risk: He had worn the King's uniform most of his life, yet the man himself was nothing of a soldier.

As a finale, the bombardment of Roxbury fizzled: the houses were too far apart, and there was not enough wind to start a satisfactory conflagration.[10]

Meanwhile, the British established themselves on the Charlestown Peninsula. With the wounded and prisoners collected, details spent the 18th gathering and burying the dead, and fortifying Bunker's Hill. When Warren's body was recognized, an angry British captain ".. stuffed the scoundrell with another Rebel into one hole and there he and his seditious principles may remain."[11] Howe's men got their tents set up on the evening of the 18th ".. except the Light Infantry, who had to guard the Works." On the 20th four women per company were allowed ".. to go to the Troops on the Charlestown side." Predictably, on the 21st there was an order against women ".. selling or giving Rum to the Soldiers." By the 26th Howe was ordering that the men ".. Bathe in the Salt Water Mornings and Evenings when the Tide admitts ...", with suitable precautions, as "Salutary" for their health.[12]

Both sides prepared their official versions of the battle. Nonchalant as ever, Gage did not make out his report to Lord Dorchester of the Colonial Office until 25 June. It was bland, detached, short, and largely a copying of Howe's report of 21 June.

Captain Chadds of the *Cerberus* brought it to London on 25 July. The Lords Commissioners of the Admiralty graciously supplemented it on 27 July by furnishing Dartmouth copies of Graves' last three letters. (A bit of carelessness now brought Gage unneeded trouble. Howe had praised Clinton for coming ". . a Volunteer into the action . . ." and inspiring the troops. In Gage's rewording, Clinton assisted Howe but ". . followed the re-enforcement." Clinton, who had gone ahead of those troops (See Chapter XIII) and had been worrying over the possibility of being disciplined for leaving his assigned post to do so, chose to consider this phrase a reflection on his courage, and bombarded Gage with outraged letters.)

Gage's personal correspondence for once, however, held something of real hurt and sense of failure. "My Lord, you will receive an account of some success against the Rebels, but attended with a long list of killed and wounded, so many of the latter that the hospital hardly has hands sufficient to take care of them . . . These people shew a Spirit and Conduct against us they never shewed against the French, and every body has Judged of them from their former appearance and behavior when joyned with the Kings Forces in the last War; which has led many into great mistakes. They are now spirited up by a Rage and Enthousiasm, as great as ever People were possessed of, and you must proceed in earnest or give the Business up . . . The loss we have Sustained is greater than we can bear. Small Army's cant afford such losses . . . I wish this Cursed place was burned. Its only use is its harbor . . ."[13]

His subordinates agreed with him. It had been a victory but—as Howe put it—". . The success is too dearly bought." The Americans had fought far better than expected, had used the terrain efficiently, had shown a surprising skill in improvising fortifications. (Few Englishmen seemed to have guessed the numbers of Americans who had, one way or another, refused to fight.) They knew that their own planning had been bad, that their artillery had failed them inexcusably. To most of them the battle had been one single assault—driving forward, recoiling, and then surging triumphantly over the American defenses—rather than the neat series of attacks and repulses which Americans remembered.[14]

As for the Americans, Ward submitted no report. Unlike Gage, he seems to have received none from his subordinates. The first American account of the battle was attributed to one "Elijah Hide, of Lebanon, who was a spectator on Winter's Hill during the whole action." (Winter's Hill was some two miles west of Bunker's Hill: All Hide could have seen was the smoke.) Obviously he was from Connecticut—he attributed all the virtue of the day to the Connecticut troops, and ended the battle with Putnam pursuing the British ". . until they got under the cover of their cannon from the shipping," though he did admit they later ". . returned to Bunker's Hill . . ."[15]

In July the Massachusetts Provincial Congress ordered its Committee of Safety to ". . draw up and transmitt to Great-Britain a fair & impartial account of the late Battle of Charlestown." It was to counteract ". . the advantages our enemies will derive from General Gage's misrepresentations." The Committee accordingly produced one, which on 25 July was mailed to Arthur Lee (a Virginian then serving as Massachusett's agent in London), ". . desiring you to insert the Same in the public Papers, so that the European World may be convinced of the causeless & unexampled cruelty with which the British Ministry have treated the innocent American Colonies." This rather naive document was produced by a committee of three clergymen; only one of them, the Reverend Mr. Peter Thacher, had seen anything of the battle—and that from the far bank of the Mystic River, over a mile upstream from the north end of the Rail Fence. These reverend gentlemen interviewed various officers, particularly Colonel Prescott, and presumably did their best in a task for which they were not qualified. Being from Massachusetts, they emphasized Prescott's fight around the redoubt, and made no specific mention of New Hampshire or Connecticut. Many legends concerning the battle—such as that of the three successive British frontal attacks, delivered against the entire American front, from Charlestown to the Mystic River—can be traced to their earnest labors. In one respect they really voiced American public feeling—the burning of Charlestown demanded the ". . Sacrifice of those miscreants who have introduced horror, desolation & Havock into the once happy abode of liberty, peace, & plenty." Americans had strong feelings on the sacredness of their property—there was no excuse for burning down a private house just because someone was shooting at you from its front yard or windows.[16]

Some contemporary reports were even more fraudulent than Hide's. These include the striking "An Impartial and Authentic Narrative . . ." of Lieutenant John Clarke of the marines, and the ultra-patriotic story of the Reverend John Martin. Clarke had been under arrest awaiting return to England for dismissal from the service for drunkenness, and wrote from hearsay and invention. Martin was a mysterious figure—probably a British agent—who invented his story to gain credence among the American clergy.[17]

There also are items, presumably written by Americans, which today would be classed as "black propaganda." One is a "letter from an officer on board one of the King's ships at Boston"— ". . the moment [the Americans] discovered the landing of our Troops, they formed in order of battle . . . [and] marched toward us with the utmost coolness and regularity. Nothing can exceed the panic and apparent dislike of most of the King's Troops to enter into this engagement; even at the landing, several attempted to run away, and five actually took to their heels in order to join the Americans, but were presently brought back, and two of them were immediately hung up *in terrorem* to the rest."[18]

Their writings done, the two armies prepared for the next confrontation. Gage pushed the fortification of both the Boston and Charlestown peninsulas as if he were beleaguered by Frederick the Great, with all the armed might of Prussia at his hand, rather than by Artemas Ward. Inspecting Bunker's Hill after the British evacuated Boston, Washington thought that "Twenty thousand men could not carry it against 1,000, had [it] been well defended." The fortifications of Boston Neck were even more elaborate.[19] Thus safely ensconced, Gage—now christened "Blundering Tom"—might have had men to spare for offensive action but never considered it. Probably he knew that England had found him wanting. He was recalled in late September, to spend the rest of his service in various comfortable and inconspicuous corners. Howe received command of the British forces from the Floridas to Nova Scotia. It was hoped that he could withdraw from Boston before the winter storms, preferably to New York.[20] Bad weather and a shortage of shipping prevented this movement. The British army spent another miserable winter in Boston, cold, sickly, and on short rations.

Artemas Ward had more immediate problems, the first of which was ammunition. He did not have enough to fight another battle, and there was no chance of getting more in the near future. (In August, Washington would discover that the available reserve of gunpowder would provide only nine cartridges for each soldier, and that lead and gun flints also were in critically short supply.)[21] Almost as serious was the fact that many soldiers had left blankets, coats, and other clothing and equipment on the battlefield. Without blankets, or at least coats, they had nothing to protect their muskets and ammunition against rain: ". . If . . . we should be attacked Immediately after ye rain is over," Ward wrote the Committee of Supplies, "pray what are we to Expect?" His own answer was ". . Destruction . .", but the Committee could give him neither blankets nor clothing, and relief had to come from patriotic citizens. Moreover, Bunker's Hill had been a hard lesson on the importance of the bayonet. New Hampshire troops were emphatic on that subject, asking their Committee of Safety for 500 to 1,000 bayonets as soon as possible—". . tis barbarous to let men be obliged to oppose Bayonets with only gun Barrels." As a stopgap measure Ward got the provincial Congress to provide him with 1,500 "spears" which might be used for a literally last-ditch defense of his fortifications. The latter were extended and improved from Roxbury north to the Mystic River.[22]

These material problems aside, there was the overriding concern that many Americans had been cowardly, disloyal, or incompetent. Justly, most blame was placed on the officers. "Our men are in Spirits . . ." wrote William Tudor. "We have Men enough, but want officers. We have 20,000 at least within six miles of Boston, but they are little better than an armed Mob. The Officers have too little Controul over their Men. And unless a very great Change takes Place in our Camps We never can face disciplin'd Troops on plain Ground."[23] Ward was criticized because he had not left his headquarters during the day, but even his worst critics admitted he was irreplaceable at that moment.

Investigations and court-martials went on for weeks. Mansfield lost his regiment; Scammon managed to convince his court-martial that he had honestly misunderstood his orders; Gerrish was under suspicion, but survived until he definitely played the coward in a skirmish some weeks later. The Artillery Regiment received a much-needed shake-down. Major Scarborough Gridley was dismissed in September for misconduct at Bunker's Hill; Captain John Callender was cashiered for cowardice; Captain Samuel Gridley's commission was withheld, but a court-martial acquitted him of cowardice—possibly through his father's influence. (Callender rejoined the army as a volunteer, and got his sentence revoked for gallantry at Long Island the next year.) In November a major reorganization put Colonel Henry Knox in Colonel Gridley's place as artillery commander.

After the arrival of General George Washington, with experienced assistants in Major General Charles Lee and Brigadier General Horatio Gates, the army (formally adopted by the Continental Congress as the "Continental Army" on 25 July) really began to learn drill, discipline, and professional conduct. Officers were expected to act as such or get out of the service. They must learn how to keep their men healthy—to see that they used the latrines instead of leaving their ". . Excrament about the fields Pernishously . . ."; to make certain that their rations were properly cooked, and keep bad liquor out of the camps. Above all, they must realize that this was an army, that orders were to be obeyed promptly and without quibbling, and that local loyalties must give place to new national spirit.[24]

It was a hard task, and sometimes almost a hopeless one, but its ending was lean Continental regiments that could meet British regulars in stand-up battle with the intent, hope, and reasonable expectation of breaking them. No other American soldiers have endured so terribly and so long—stark naked except for a ragged blanket about them in winter, living on ". . perfect carrion" and ". . bad as it was . . . often without any." They made flesh the old proverb: "Nothing has even been made until the soldier has made safe the field where the building shall be built, and the soldier is the scaffolding until it has been built, and the soldier gets no reward but honor."

And the beginning of that army was the men who fought at Bunker's Hill—the men with Stark, Reed, and Knowlton along the Rail Fence and the stone wall across the Mystic beach; the unknown men who held the *fleches*; the men who built and defended Prescott's redoubt; the sharpshooters hanging on in blazing Charlestown; Trevett's artillerymen working their last gun; the men who followed Gardner and Little into the lost battle to cover the retreat. They might be defeated; they were not whipped.

GLOSSARY

Advice Boat: A small, swift vessel used for carrying dispatches.

Alarm Post: A position previously designated for a particular unit to occupy in case of an alarm.

Beat to Quarters: In naval usage, a drum beat that was the signal for the crew to go to their battle stations.

Blind: A short section of breastwork built in front of an opening in the main fortifications, to block enemy fire and observation.

Cashier: (From the French *casser*, to break.) To dismiss from the military service with dishonor.

Commissary: An official (in the 18th century, a civilian) responsible for the procurement, transportation, and/or issue of rations.

Conductor: Civilian staff assistants, charged with the movement of supplies. Those of the artillery were in charge of the ammunition wagons in the field.

Drafts: (Also "draughts") Troops taken from one unit to bring another up to strength.

Ensign: The lowest grade of commissioned officer in the infantry, equivalent to the modern 2d lieutenant. So called because he originally carried the company's colors.

Express: A courier or dispatch rider, used to carry urgent orders or information.

Firelock: A flintlock musket.

Gorget: A crescent-shaped piece of metal (either silver or goldplated) worn at the throat by British officers on duty as an insignia of commissioned rank.

Guard Boat: A boat—usually from a warship—used to patrol harbors.

Guard Ship: A ship employed for coastal patrol and guard duty.

Gunfiring: Time at which the morning and evening guns were fired.

Halberd: (Also "halbert") A pole arm, usually 7 to 8½ feet in length, with a spear head, below which was an axehead-like blade and a sharp beak. It was the traditional weapon of sergeants and town watches.

Military Chest: The funds of an army, particularly cash actually available.

Rank and File: "Men carrying the firelock, and standing in the ranks." In this period, this included only privates and corporals, and was used in reckoning the effective strength of a unit. American usage of this term was frequently loose and inexact.

Returns: Reports on the state of a unit, listing the number of men on duty, leave, detached service, sick in quarters, sick in the hospital, prisoners, etc. Returns after an engagement show the number and types of casualties.

Spontoon: (Also "Espontoon") A pole arm carried by infantry officers, approximately 7 to 8 feet long. It had a simple spearhead with a short crossbar below it.

Stores: Military supplies, including food, forage, arms, ammunition, and clothing. *Naval stores* included those used for ships' repair and maintenance.

Subaltern: A commissioned officer below the grade of captain—a lieutenant or ensign.

Tender: A small vessel employed as an auxiliary to larger warships: Tenders might be employed for reconnaissance, carrying extra supplies, or utility work around harbors.

Train, Artillery: All the artillery belonging to an army in the field.

Watch, Town: A municipal police force, composed of "watchmen."

BIBLIOGRAPHY

Books listed here are major references.
Books used only for specific chapters
are mentioned in their Notes.

Short Title	
Adm.	*Admiralty Records*. Public Records Office, London.
Barker	*The Diary of Lieutenant John Barker, 4th (or the King's Own) Regiment of Foot, From November, 1774, to May, 1776. Journal of the Society for Army Historical Research,* London, 1928, 81-109, 145-174. This printing also contains appropriate excerpts from Howe's Orderly Book.
Berniere MS.	Bernière, Henry de. *Account of Reconnaissances, 1775. Journal of the Society for Army Historical Research,* London, 1928, 170-174. Supposedly, this account was found in Boston after the British evacuation, and printed by Americans in 1779. However, it appears thoroughly factual.
Berniere map	Bernière, Henry de. *Sketch of the action on the Heights of Charlestown June 17th, 1775 between His Majesty's troops under the command of Major Genl. Howe, and a large body of American rebels. Copied by I. A. Chapman from an original sketch taken by Henry De. Berniere of the 14th Regiment of Infantry, now in the hands of J. Cist, esq.* Library of Congress G3701.S3143 1775 .D4 181- This copy is in the same crude style of known De Berniere maps. A much modified version of this copy carries the same title except for the following addition: "Engraved by Kneass, Young & Co. for the Analectic magazine. Philada, M. Thomas."
Bouton	Bouton, Nathaniel (Ed.) *Provincial Papers: Documents and Records Relating to the Province of New Hampshire from 1764 to 1776.* 7 vols., Concord, 1867-1873.
Clinton	*Clinton Manuscripts.* William L. Clements Library, Ann Arbor, Michigan. Clinton's horrible handwriting and odd sentence structure frequently make it difficult to comprehend his exact meaning; conscientious readers may well differ over the correct "translation." Clinton, Sir Henry. *The American Rebellion: Sir Henry Clinton's Narrative of His Campaigns, 1775-1782, With an Appendix of Original Documents.* Yale University Press, 1954. An excellent edition, edited by William B. Willcox. It contains very little on the battle, but is invaluable for a study of Clinton himself.
Coffin	Coffin, Charles (Ed.) *History of the Battle of Breed's Hill, by Major-Generals William Heath, Henry Lee, James Wilkinson, and Henry Dearborn.* Saco, Maine, 1831. Heath was at Roxbury during the battle; however, he wrote from notes made during the period. Lee had no first-hand knowledge whatever. Wilkinson wrote late (1816), based on his memories of visiting the area in 1776; his account is spiked with propaganda against Winfield Scott and other personal enemies. Dearborn fought at the Rail Fence, but also wrote late (1818) and used his version as a politically motivated attack on Putnam. This edition includes a number of accounts by other veterans of the battle, apparently added to support Dearborn.
CHSC	*Collections of the Connecticut Historical Society.* Hartford, 1860.
C.O.	*Colonial Office Records,* London.
Dawson	Dawson, Henry B. (Ed.) *Historical Magazine,* June, 1868. Morrisania, New York.
Drake	Drake, Samuel A. (Ed.) *Bunker Hill: The Story Told in Letters from the Battle Field by British Officers Engaged.* Boston, 1875.
Fonblanque	Fonblanque, E. D. de. *Political and Military Episodes . . . Derived From the Life and Correspondence of the Right Hon. J. Burgoyne.* 2 vols, London, 1876. Much original material.
Force	Force, Peter. *American Archives, Series 4.* An invaluable collection of original documents.
Ford	Ford, Worthington C. (Ed.) *Journals of the Continental Congress.* 34 vols., Washington, 1904-1937.
Freeman	Freeman, Douglas S. *George Washington: Volume Three, Planter and Patriot.* New York, 1948.
French	French, Allen. *The First Year of the American Revolution.* Boston, 1934. This book is the product of skilled research and excellent writing. Unfortunately, the author had neither practical knowledge nor judgement of military matters.
Frothingham	Frothingham, Richard. *History of the Siege of Boston.* Boston, 1849. Old, but valuable, if used with care.
Gage	*Gage Manuscripts.* William L. Clements Library, Ann Arbor, Michigan.
Gage Corr.	Carter, Clarence E. (Ed.) *The Correspondence of General Thomas Gage . . . 1763-1775.* 2 vols., New Haven, 1931-1933. A sketchy selection from the MSS.
Geo. III Corr.	Fortescue, John W. (Ed.) *The Correspondence of King George the Third from 1760 to December, 1783.* 6 vols., London, 1927-1928.
Graves	Graves, Samuel. *Graves's Conduct.* Massachusetts Historical Society Transcript. An essential source, but inexplicably neglected. (See USN.)
Harris	Harris, George. *Life and Services of General Lord Harris.* London, 1840.
Heath	Heath, William. *Memoirs of Major-General Heath, Containing Anecdotes, Details of Skirmishes, Battles, and Other Military Events During the American War. Written by Himself.*

	Boston, 1798.
Howe	Howe, General Sir William. *Orderly Book at Charlestown, Boston, and Halifax*. London, 1890. Edited by Benjamin F. Stevens.
Kemble	Kemble, Stephen. *The Kemble Papers*. 2 vols., New York, 1883-1884. Kemble was "Deputy-Adjutant-General of the Forces in North America." His major qualification for this post seems to have been the fact that he also was Gage's brother-in-law.
Lincoln	Lincoln, William (Ed.) *Journals of Each Provincial Congress of Massachusetts*. Boston, 1838. According to Lincoln, these *Journals* were far from complete when he compiled them, a number of items having disappeared or possibly been altered.
Lister	Innes, R. A. *Jeremy Lister, 10th Regiment, 1770-1783. Journal of the Society for Army Historical Research*, London, 1963, 59-73.
LO	Loudoun, John, Earl of. *Loudoun Papers*. Henry E. Huntington Library, San Marino, California.
Mackenzie	Mackenzie, Frederick. *A British Fusilier in Revolutionary Boston, Being the Diary of Lieutenant Frederick Mackenzie, Adjutant of the Royal Welch Fusiliers, January 5-April 30, 1775*. Cambridge, 1926. Carefully edited by Allen French.
Martyn	Martyn, Charles. *The Life of Artemus Ward*. New York, 1921.
MHS	Massachusetts Historical Society. *The Battle of Bunker Hill*. Boston, 1968.
MHSP	Massachusetts Historical Society. *Proceedings*.
Montresor	Scull, G. D., (Ed.) *The Montresor Journals*. New York, 1881. Unfortunately, Montresor's papers for the period of Bunker's Hill were lost.
Murdock	Murdock, Harold. *Bunker Hill: Notes and Queries on a Famous Battle*. Boston, 1927. Invaluable, both for factual content and as an example of historical research.
NHHS	New Hampshire Historical Society. *Collections*.
NR	*Niles Register*, Vol. 14, page 179. Baltimore. Contains Washington's story of Braddock's defeat, as told to a friend.
Pargellis	Pargellis, Stanley McC. *Lord Loudoun in North America*. Yale University, 1968.
Parker	Parker, Francis J. *Colonel William Prescott, The Commander in the Battle of Bunker's Hill*. Boston, 1875. Typical of the partisan descriptions of the battle produced by supporters of both Prescott and Putnam.
Percy	Bolton, Charles K. (Ed.) *Letters of Hugh Earl Percy from Boston and New York, 1774-1776*. Boston, 1902.
Pomeroy	Forest, Louis E. de (Ed.) *The Journals and Papers of Seth Pomeroy*. New York, 1926.
Rawdon	British Historical Manuscripts Commission. *Hastings Manuscripts*, Vol. III, 154-155. London, 1934.
Shy	Shy, John. *Toward Lexington*. Princeton, 1965.
USN	Clark, William B. (Ed.) U.S. Navy History Division. *Naval Documents of the American Revolution*, Vols. I and II. Washington, 1964. An essential, well-organized source for naval

	activities of this period.
Wade	Wade, Herbert T. and Robert A. Lively (Eds.) *This Glorious Cause*. Princeton, 1958. The wartime letters of two Massachusetts officers.
Ward	Ward, Christopher. *The War of the Revolution*. 2 vols., New York, 1952. Recent research has developed many errors in this work, but it remains highly useful.
Williams	*Discord and Civil Wars, Being a Portion of the Journal Kept by Lieutenant Williams of His Majesty's Twenty-Third Regiment while Stationed in British North America During the Time of the Revolution*. Buffalo, 1954.
W.O.	War Office, London.

NOTES

CHAPTER I

THE HOSTILE SHORE

(1) Edited by Samuel A. Green, Boston, for private distribution, 1872.

(2) Ellis, Kenneth. *The Post Office in the Eighteenth Century*, London, 1958, 96.

(3) Wood, William. *New England's Prospect*, 1634. (From Shurtleff, Nathaniel B. *Topographical and Historical Description of Boston*, Boston, 1872.) During the last century, most of the dangerous reefs in Boston harbor and its approaches have been removed; the rest have been marked.

(4) *Percy*, 45.

(5) *Barker*, 87; *Adm*. 1/485.

(6) *Percy*, 55.

(7) *Barker*, 87, 107, 157.

(8) According to Boston tradition, the pilot thereafter became a sexton, but was haunted by the verse frequently chalked on his door "Don't you run this church ashore, like you did that seventy-four."

(9) Snow, Edward R. *Two Forts Named Independence*, Braintree, Mass., 1967. Because of the filling in of Boston harbor, the fort's site is now the tip of a peninsula. Its name was changed to "Fort Independence" in 1776. With its 210 guns, including massive 42-pounders, it was probably the strongest fort in North America.

(10) Local terminology of this period frequently is confusing. "Dorchester Neck," for example, might refer either to the narrow isthmus of that peninsula, or to the entire peninsula.

(11) Pares, Richard. *War and Trade in the West Indies*, London, 1936; especially 394-468.

(12) Whitehall, Walter M. *Boston, A Topographical History*, Cambridge, Mass., 1963, 29, 37-38, 213-214.

(13) *Barker*, 91. *Sandwich*, I, 59-62.

(14) *Williams*, 5.

(15) *Whitehall*, 7 (see 12, above). *Barker*, 101.

(16) *Shy*, 303-320, 407-418. *Williams*, 7-9.

(17) *Barker*, 85.

(18) *Lister*, 61.

(19) *Lister*, 61-62. *Barker*, 83, 93.

(20) *Gage MSS*, June 1774.

(21) *Barker*, 83.

(22) *Barker*, 101, 103.

(23) *Barker*, 95. *Mackenzie*.

(24) *Percy*, 38 - 12 Sept. 1744. See also Shy, John W. *A New Look at Colonial Militia, William and Mary Quarterly*, April 1963.

(25) *Percy*, 58-59.

CHAPTER II
THE NONCHALANT GENERAL

(1) *LO*: 6153, 6223, and 6250.
(2) *Encyclopedia Britannica.*
(3) *NR*, Volume 14, 179. Probably the best analysis of Braddock's defeat at the Monongahela is: Yaple, Robert L. *"Braddock's Defeat: The Theories and a Reconsideration,"* *Journal of the Society for Army Historical Research*, Winter, 1968, 194-201.
(4) *LO*: 5065, 5072, 5074, 5075. W.O.: 34, 72.
(5) A good account of this campaign is in O'Conor, Norris J., *A Servant of the Crown*, New York, 1938, based on the papers of John Appy, Secretary and Judge Advocate of His Majesty's Forces in North America. (Also, Webster, J.C. (editor) *The Journal of Jeffery Amherst*, Chicago, 1931, 171.)
(6) *LO*: 6133, 6135, 6137.
(7) *Gage. Kemble*, I, 1.
(8) Gage's continual hostilities with Rogers are covered in Cuneo, John R. *Robert Rogers of the Rangers*, New York, 1959 (thoroughly based on the Gage MSS and Colonial Office records). His feud with Bradstreet is partially covered in *Shy*. Neither Bradstreet nor Rogers were particularly saintly, but both were daring, efficient combat officers, and Bradstreet was a logistical genius.
(9) *Geo. III Corr.* III, #1379.
(10) *Gage Corr.* I, 371-375.
(11) *Percy*, 38. *Barker*, 83. *Williams*, 9-10.
(12) *Mackenzie*, 39.
(13) *Barker*, 85. Concurrently, American wit dubbed Gage "Mother Cary."
(14) *Barker*, 84, 89-91.
(15) *Berniere*, 170-174. These officers found that an offer of *tea* indicated a friendly loyalist household, but were hampered by not being able to move on Sundays.
(16) *CO*: 5:91 and 5:92. (William Legge, Earl of Dartmouth.)
(17) *Gage,* especially letters to Sir Guy Carleton, 3 June 1775, and to William Wildman, Viscount Barrington, Secretary at War, 12 June 1775.
(18) *Gage Corr.* II, 179-183.
(19) *Barker*, 98-101.
(20) *Graves*. I, 73, 74. Roxbury Heights commanded the western approaches to the Boston and Dorchester "necks."
(21) *Geo. III Corr.* III, 215-216.
(22) For an uncritical history of Gage, read Alden, John R. *General Gage in America*, Baton Rouge, 1948.

CHAPTER III
THE FRUSTRATED GENERAL

(1) British admirals were designated, according to their seniority within their respective grades, as "Red" (senior), "White", and "Blue".
(2) *British Museum*, Ms. 14038: 1:46v. *Adm.* 51/218 and 51/804.
(3) *Percy*, 65.
(4) *Percy*, 60. (12 Aug. 1775).
(5) This statement is based on the evidence of the *Gage* papers and *Admiralty* records.
(6) *Barker*, 101.
(7) *Gage. Graves*, Appen., 416. *Adm.* 51/804. *Mass. Archives*, Vol. 138, 428.
(8) *Graves*, I, 103, 104.

(9) *Graves*, I, 70.
(10) *Graves*, I, 78 and Appen. 407, 408.
(11) *Barker*, 108a.
(12) *Gage* (19 May). *Graves*, I, 108. (General George Washington later planned just such a whaleboat assault across the Back Bay, as a counterattack, if the British attacked his new fortifications on Dorchester Heights.)
(13) *Graves*, I, 74, 75, 79-81.
(14) *Graves*, I, 135, 136, 153-156. Also *Williams*, 25.
(15) *Adm.*, 1/485. *Graves*, I, 129, 130.
(16) *Adm.*, 1/485; 51/663; 51/867; 51/4136; 51/4330; 52/7746. *Graves*, I, 55-60, 62, 83-86, 92. *Gage.*
(17) *Graves*, I, 41. (The names of these ships are variously spelled, and the number of their guns varies somewhat in different accounts.)
(18) *Graves*, I, 63-67, 88, 89, 96-98; II, 191; Appen. 443, 462, 463. *Gage.*
(19) *Graves*, I, 90-92. *Gage. CO*, Class 5/92.
(20) *Graves*, I, 51, 54, 55-60, 88, 89, 108, 129, 179, 181. *Adm.* 51/336.
(21) *Adm.* 51/867. *Graves*, 108, 129.
(22) *Adm.* 2/99, 2/259.
(23) *Adm.* 1/485, 2/99/261, 2/99/283, 2/548, 2/284. *Graves*, I, 83, 92, 103, 104. *Mass. Archives*, Vol. 138, 428.
(24) *Graves*, I, 165, 168. (A total of 350 men had been thus detailed.)
(25) *CO*, Class 5/92. *Barker*, 87.
(26) *Gage.*
(27) *Gage.*
(28) *Graves*, I, 138. *Gage.*
(29) *Barker. Gage. Graves*, I, 138. The "Engineer's Carpenters" were civilian artificers employed by Gage's Engineer officer, Lieutenant John Montresor.

CHAPTER IV
THE EMBATTLED FARMERS

(1) *Martyn. Lincoln*, 35. Ward's "stone" apparently was a gallstone, which would make any violent exercise such as riding extremely painful.
(2) *Force*, 4, II, 384.
(3) Jedediah Huntington to Jonathan Trumbull: *Trumbull Papers*, Force Transcript, Library of Congress.
(4) *Freeman*, III, 544-552.
(5) *Lincoln*, 230.
(6) *Pomeroy*, 166-167.
(7) *Bouquet and Haldimand Papers*, No. 21, 634. British Museum.
(8) *Lincoln*, 148, 519-521.
(9) *Lincoln*, 143, 152, 519-521, 522, 523.
(10) *Force*, 4, II, 813, 1350-1351, 1413-1414. *Lincoln*, 292, 295, 339, 342, 347, 400-401, 462, 531, 534-536, 664, 694, 716-718.
(11) *Mass. Archives*, 193:69.
(12) *Force*, 4, II, 647.
(13) *Lincoln*, 258, 325, 562-563. *Force*, 4, II, 813-814, 1350-1351, 1413-1414. *Frothingham*, 118n.
(14) *Force*, 4, I, 1347; 4, II, 315-316, 611, 748, 1049-1050, 1372, 1397. *Lincoln*, 118, 453. Smith, Samuel S. (Ed.) *At General Howe's Side, 1776-1778*. Monmouth Beach, N.J., 1974, 39. *Kemble,* I, 514. On 30 April Mackenzie noticed a party of Indians in Charlestown, but their presence at the battle of Bunker's Hill cannot be positively established. Several Negro soldiers served under Prescott in the fighting around the redoubt, and seem to have done as well as their White comrades.

(15) *Lincoln*, 35, 65, 325, 326, 333. *Mass. Archives*, Vol. 194. *Pomeroy*. *Force*, 4, II, 1414.

(16) *Lincoln*, 141-142, 157, 213-214, 220, 232, 373, 511, 515. *Force*, 4, II, 894.

(17) *Force*, 4, II, 386.

(18) *Force*, 4, II, 1349-1350. Sargent was attempting to recruit additional companies. Reed's name often is spelled "Reid" or "Read." The exact history of his regiment is uncertain. Most of it may have been raised in New Hampshire.

(19) *Bouton*, VII, 474-484, 493. *NHHS*, VII, 1.

(20) *Bouton*, VII, 495-496, 503. *NHHS*, VII, 3. Stark was the last colonel so approved, which left him junior to Poor and Reed but commanding the senior (1st) regiment. Sargent seems to have been favored by the Massachusetts Committee of Safety, but few of the New Hampshiremen around Boston would enlist with him. See *Force*, 4, II, 386.

(21) *NHHS*, VII, 6. *Force*, 4, II, 639-640, 1069-1070, 1092, 1529. *Dawson*, 331. Stark, standing on his Massachusetts commission (all record of which has disappeared), initially refused to acknowledge Folsom's authority.

(22) *Force*, 4, II, 868. Unlike the older New England colonies, New Hampshire was settled in considerable part by Scots-Irish. See Cuneo, John R., *Robert Rogers of the Rangers*, New York, 1959; 4-5, 9-10, 33-34.

(23) *Records of Connecticut*, XIV, 417. These regiments had ten companies. Their field officers also commanded companies.

(24) *USN*, I, 520. *Ford*, II, 95.

(25) *Records of Connecticut*, XV, 85, 87-89. *Force*, 4, II, 414-417.

(26) *Dawson*, June 1868, 387. The Rhode Island artillery had a brown uniform with red facings. A good many officers had uniforms of one kind or another.

(27) These were provincial rangers, considered several cuts below Rogers' Rangers who were semi-regulars.

(28) Bowen, Clarence W. *The History of Woodstock, Conn.*, Woodstock, 1926, 117-118.

(29) *Force*, 4, II, 1145, 1147-1148.

(30) *Force*, 4, II, 894.

(31) *Force*, 4, II, 1143, 1152.

(32) Letter by the Rev. William Emerson, *French*, 300.

(33) Samuel Grey, a resident of Roxbury, *Frothingham*, 394.

(34) *Lincoln*, 563.

(35) *Force*, 4, II, 664, 676.

(36) See *Ward*, I, 50, for an interesting study of American marksmanship at Lexington/Concord. A similar computation will show that Americans did not shoot much straighter at Bunker's Hill.

(37) *Force*, 4, II, 1029, 1472-1473. See also the graphic, if biased, account by the Loyalist agent, Benjamin Thompson, *Stopford-Sackville MSS*, H.M. Stationery Office, London, II, 15-18, which emphasizes the fact that the Americans went dirty in part for lack of female camp followers.

CHAPTER V
THE KING'S BAD BARGAINS

(1) *Barker*, 89, 92.

(2) *Shy*, 413-415. *Barker*, 88, 94.

(3) Lawson, Cecil C.P. *A History of the Uniforms of the British Army*, Vol. II, London, 1941, 46. As the junior elite unit, the light infantry company formed on the left of the regimental line.

(4) *Barker*, 96. Barker thought it was "a blind" to conceal preparations for a future operation but Mackenzie who was in charge of the light infantry training, appeared to consider it routine.

(5) *Inspection Return*, 7 April 1774. *Journal of the Society for Army Historical Research*, January-March, 1925, 33.

(6) *Barker*, 86, 108A, 108B, 109, 145. (Barker was a light infantry officer.) The flank companies at this time appear to have had 39 privates and corporals. For an excellent analysis of this custom, see Marshal Saxe's remarks in Phillips, Thomas R. (editor), *Roots of Strategy*, Harrisburg, 1940, 215.

(7) The "Incorporated Corps" eventually consisted of the grenadiers and two battalion companies of the 18th and six companies of the 65th.

(8) *Percy*, 36. *Barker*, 87, 88, 89-90.

(9) *Germain Papers*, William L. Clements Library, Ann Arbor, Mich. 40 officers and 26 noncommissioned officers were to accompany these recruits as replacements. The 17th Light Dragoons sent their regimental quartermaster ahead in mid-April. *Correspondence Politique, Angleterre*, Bibliotheque Nationale, Paris, Vol. 508, 251; Vol. 509, 262.

(10) *Williams*, 3-4 *W.O.*, 36/1, K 212. *Barker*, 107.

(11) *Gage*. *Graves*, I, 42-48, 55-60. *Sandwich Papers*, Navy Records Society, London, I, 57-62. (Pitcairn corresponded directly with the First Lord of the Admiralty.)

(12) *Adm.* 2/1168. *Drake*, 74. *C.O.*, Class 5/92.

(13) *W.O.* 36/3, K 212. *Barker*, 103.

(14) *Barker*, 92, 102, 108. *C.O.*, Class 5/92.

(15) See Savory, Reginald, *His Britannic Majesty's Army in Germany*, Oxford, 1966, especially 166-169, 181.

(16) *W.O.*, 10/143-146. Also *Battery Records of the Royal Artillery, 1716-1859*, Royal Artillery Institute, 1952, 46. A fifth company, usually included by historians, did not reach Boston until the last of June.

(17) *Barker*, 83, 108.

(18) James, Charles. *A Universal Military Dictionary*, London, 1816, 27.

(19) *Dawson*, 368.

(20) *Lister*, 66.

(21) *Montresor*, 418. *Kemble*, I, 74. *Force*, 5, IV, 423, 484.

(22) Connolly, T.W.J. *The History of the Royal Corps of Sappers and Miners*, London, 1855.

(23) *The Montresor Journals* contain James Montresor's American journals for 1757-1759, as well as John Montresor's. Unfortunately, the section of the latter dealing with Boston, 1775, was lost. James Montresor himself apparently had no formal training, and was not considered capable of conducting a siege. See *Pargellis*, 318-320.

(24) *Mackenzie*, 27. *Barker*, 87, 91, 97. *Harris*, 18.

(25) *Barker*, 100, 104, 109. *Additional Manuscript*, 38208, f. 180, British Museum.

(26) *Gage*. *C.O.*, *Gage-Dartmouth Correspondence*, Historical MSS Commission, London. 5:91 and 5:92. *Montresor*, 135. *Barker*, 104. (This shows what detailed knowledge the British had of Ward's Army.) *Dawson*, 368. French, Allen, *General Gage's Informers*, Ann Arbor, 1932, is an excellent reference. Dr. Church is covered in detail in *Freeman*, III, 544-552.

(27) *W.O.* 36/1, K 212. *Barker*, 86, 87, 101. Mackenzie mentions the use of "marksmen" in covering Percy's disengagement at Lexington on 19 April. *Williams*, 21-22. (Williams had joined the 23d Foot.)

* * *

CHAPTER VI
THE COMING OF THE MAJOR GENERALS

(1) *Correspondence and Proceedings*, Massachusetts Provincial Congress, Mass. Hist. Soc., April 1775. *Force*, 4, II, 370-814. *Barker*, 101, 103. *Dawson*, 376. Lieutenant Barker expressed pity for families leaving Boston ".. for half of them don't know where to go to . . ."

(2) *Howe*, 160. A company of "Royal North British Volunteers" had volunteered for such duty in October, but these were Scottish merchants and their employees—not Loyalists.

(3) *Lincoln*, 525, 526. *Force*, 4, II, 753.

(4) *Artemas Ward MSS*, Mass. Hist. Soc. *Thomas MSS*. Letter 18 May, Mass. Hist. Soc.

(5) *Warren-Adams Letters,* Mass. Hist. Soc., I, 68. *Barker*, 104. The soldierly appearance of Thomas's camp may have been due to the fact that Greene's Rhode Island troops made up a considerable part of his command as much as to his own abilities.

(6) Willard, Margaret W. *Letters on the American Revolution*, Boston, 1925, 108-109.

(7) *Barker*, 105.

(8) *Dawson*, 322.

(9) *Barker*, 106. Barker commented ".. I don't hear that he has been as fond of reconnoitering since." Hazy tradition has it that Abercrombie damned the concealed Americans for a pack of cowards, and that, when he was hit at Bunker's Hill, Americans yelled "Colonel Abercrombie, are the Yankees cowards now?"

(10) William Howe was a younger brother of George Howe, killed (1758) at Ticonderoga, and of Admiral Richard ("Black Dick") Howe.

(11) *Kemble*, 139. Kemble obviously did not like Clinton, but Clinton's constant indecision later in the war is confirmation enough of this description.

(12) For Burgoyne's opinions in his own words, see *Fonblanque*.

(13) *Barker*, 101, 102, 108. As another example of time and space factors in this war, the generals sailed from Portsmouth on 20 April, after leaving London on the 15th. (French intelligence watched them carefully.) They arrived in Boston on 25 May after an easy crossing in a fast frigate. Their horses and baggage had been sent ahead of them by transport, reaching Boston on 23 May after a 6-weeks' voyage. *Adm.* 51/663.

(14) The old story is that when Burgoyne was brought to Boston after his capture at Saratoga in 1777, he was greeted with shouts of "Give him elbow-room!"

(15) *Barker*, 106.

(16) *Force*, 4, II, 763.

(17) *Gage MSS. Kemble, I, 43. Adm.* 51/720. *Barker*, 107-109, 145. The British failure to secure this livestock is—from this distance—inexplicable. The easy way out was to damn Graves, but Gage was the commander in chief and so actually responsible. Possibly he was reluctant to seize private property; probably his staff had never considered the problem. Barker, always quick to criticize, and complaining of salt rations, seems unaware that the livestock was available for whichever side acted first. Historically, foraging—as compared to looting—never was a major talent of the British soldier.

(18) *Force*, 4, II, 1017.

* * *

CHAPTER VII
THE SAFETY OF THE COLONY

(1) *Force*, 4, II, 968-970. *Barker*, 145. *Dawson*, 3—5. For an American parody, see *Dawson*, 1-10.

(2) *MHSP*, XIV, 286.

(3) *Force*, 4, 11, 814, 823-830, 1350-1351, 1413-1414, 1629-1630. *Lincoln*, 552-577. *Frothingham*, 118n. See also Chapter IV and Appendix III.

(4) *Geo III Corr.*, 3:220. *Report of the Bunker Hill Monument Association*, 1907, 115.

(5) *Force*, 4, II, 1354. In this resolution, "Dorchester Neck" was used in the sense of the whole Dorchester Peninsula.

(6) *Freeman*, III, 551n. *Gage MSS*.

(7) *Pomeroy*, 163-164. Nevertheless, folklore has him attend this council, and support Putnam.

(8) *Ward*, I, 74, 440.

(9) Major Thomas Knowlton's rangers used it for a successful night raid in January 1776.

(10) *Dawson*, 390-391.

(11) *Dawson*, 51, 71. It is not clear whether the artillery accompanied the column or followed later after first light.

(12) *Coffin*, 396-398.

(13) *Dawson*, 385. The origin of this story seems to be Samuel Grey (a local civilian interested in military events) who said that he had gotten it second-hand.

(14) The dimensions and the design of this redoubt are variously described. *Frothingham*, 135, says that there was a sallyport (narrow opening) at the southeast corner, protected by a blind. Peter Brown of Prescott's regiment said the redoubt was "ten rod long, and eight wide."

(15) Mr. David Ludlum of the American Meteorological Society states: "It would seem that the moon on 17 June was four days past full. I have no report of cloudy weather at this time. But, on the other hand, I have found no mention of bright moonlight in the scanty firsthand material available." Bright moonlight certainly would have revealed Prescott's men. However, moonrise had been at approximately 11 o'clock on 16 June so that the moon probably was low or had set by midnight.

(16) *Clinton*. Clinton's story may be exaggerated, or even invented, but it should be considered. *Geo. III Corr.*, 3:221.

CHAPTER VIII
THE TEN OLDEST COMPANIES

(1) *Adm.* 1/485. Bishop had refused to turn the salvaged property over to Lt. Thomas Graves, one of the admiral's nephews. The average Royal Navy officer of this period had a quick eye and hand for such incidental profits.

(2) Accounts of naval actions in this and the following chapters are taken from Graves' *Conduct* and from the logs of the following vessels: *Lively - Adm.* 51/546. *Somerset - Adm.* 51/906. *Preston - Adm.* 51/720, *Adm.* 52/1921. *Glasgow - Adm.* 51/398, *Adm.* 52/1762. *Falcon - Adm.* 51/336. *Cerberus - Adm.* 51/181. *Boyne - Adm.* 52/1612. No log has been found for the *Symmetry*.

(3) Ludlum, David M. *The Weather of American Independence: the War Begins. Weatherwise*, August, 1973, 156-159. During the day the breeze shifted around to the southwest, but this hardly could have been an improvement. The *Glasgow* and *Boyne* noted periods of northerly breeze.

(4) There was no permanent grade of brigadier general in the British Army at this time. Instead, senior officers acting in that capacity might be given the temporary rank of brigadier general, usually expressed as "brigadier." Percy held the permanent grade of Colonel of the 5th Foot; Pigot and Jones were lieutenant colonels, commanding respectively the 38th Foot and the 52d Foot. (Many colonelcies were sinecures so that the lieutenant colonels were the actual commanders.)

(5) *Stopford-Sackville MSS.* Letter to Admiral Howe, 22 June 1775.

(6) Ames, Nathaniel. *An Astronomical Diary; or, an Almanack for the Year of Our Lord 1775*, Boston, 1774. Howe understood it would be at 2:00 PM.

(7) Another factor could have been the *Spitfire's* weak armament, and the fact that the *Symmetry*—as demonstrated by her performance during the 17th—was not an efficient ship.

(8) *Barker*, 105.

(9) House-to-house fighting requires special training which these troops did not have. Generally speaking, 18th century generals tried to avoid it, since they would have difficulty maintaining control of their troops—men tended to seize the plentiful opportunities to straggle, loot, and get drunk.

(10) Clinton meant that the redoubt was incomplete. A redoubt built by a professional military engineer would have had entrenched batteries to cover its flanks. The redoubt itself would be surrounded by a *ditch*, which served the function of a medieval moat. *Palisades* were strong stakes ". . about 9 feet long, fixed 3 [feet] deep in the ground, . . about 6 inches [apart]." Planted in the bottom of the ditch, these made it impossible to rush the redoubt. Pickets were shorter stakes, used to hold down the sections of sod with which a completed fortification would be faced.

(11) *Fonblanque*, 125-149, 155. *Dawson*, 66-67. Burgoyne was an expert at subtly disparaging his superiors, but his description of Gage seems accurate enough ". . capable of figuring upon ordinary and given lines of conduct, but his mind has not the resources for great, and sudden and hardy exertions . . ."

(12) *Howe's Orderly Book.* There is a shorter version in *W.O.* 36/1, which does not cover the pioneers.

(13) Letter, Cleaveland to Amherst, 3 December 1775.

(14) *Percy*, 56-57.

(15) *Ward*, I, 89. Richard M. Ketchum, *The Battle for Bunker Hill*, 96, raises the ante to "125 pounds."

(16) *W.O.*, 36/1. See James, Alfred P. and Charles M. Stotz, *Drums in the Forest*, Pittsburgh, 1958, 105, for an itemized list of the weight carried by a grenadier. Also Anburey, Thomas, *Travels Through the Interior Parts of America*, Vol. 1, 335. Officers also carried rolled blankets. Capt. Harris threw his off before the last attack, and then felt the need of it when in shock from his head wound.

(17) *Barker*, 102. *Rawdon.*

(18) Willson, Beckles (editor). *The Life and Letters of James Wolfe*, London, 1909, 392. By one of history's ironies, Wolfe wrote this to his former colonel, Lord George Sackville who—as Lord George Germain—soon would take over direction of the British war effort. Germain (whom the same description would have fitted rather well) knew nothing of America, but apparently judged Americans by Wolfe's description. Wolfe himself had been very glad to have Major Joseph Gorham's six-company "corps of rangers" at Quebec.

(19) *Williams*, 17. *Dawson*, 338. *Rawdon.* There is no agreement as to the number and type of cannon in action here. On a guess, there might have been six 24-pounders, three howitzers, and one mortar.

(20) "Warping" was employed in calms or close waters. It was accomplished by sending a boat with a light anchor (or "kedge") out to the full length of the anchor cable where it was dropped. The ship's crew then took up the cable on its capstan, hauling the ship forward. For speed, two boats and two kedge anchors might be used.

(21) A "spring on the cable" was a nautical trick for turning a ship. A ship, with its bow anchor down, would fasten a cable from its stern to the anchor cable. Hauling on the stern cable would wind the ship around.

(22) *Clinton.*

CHAPTER IX
UNDER A VERY WARM FIRE

(1) *Martyn*, opposite page 124. Orderly Book of Sgt. Nathan Stow, Nixon's Regt. Public Library, Concord, Mass. *CHSC*, VII, 22.

(2) *Dawson,* 390-391. Prescott's only known personal description of the battle is in the letter used here which he wrote to John Adams on 25 August. It is a bad-tempered document, which deals harshly with other Americans who also served honorably, and so should be taken with more than one grain of salt.

(3) James, Charles. *An Universal Military Dictionary,* London, 1816, 723. "Redoubt . . . a square work . . . having loop holes for the small arms to fire through, and being surrounded by a ditch." (This redoubt never was completed, and so had no loopholes.) Batteries were three-sided works, left open to the rear so that it was easier to get guns into and out of them and so that—if captured—they would give the enemy no protection.

(4) Gridley was aging and may have needed some rest; probably he went back to bring up the artillery. It was not loss of nerve—he returned later and was wounded.

(5) *Coffin*, 376. *Dawson*, 381-384, 390.

(6) *Dawson*, 376-378. This undoubtedly is the William Tudor who served as Judge Advocate at Col. Scammon's court-martial (See Chapter XV). What—except curiosity—would bring him to Breed's Hill is a puzzle, but Prescott may have been bothered by a good many such unnecessary rubbernecks. Tudor's statement is valuable since it suggests that the Americans actually did plan to emplace heavy artillery on Breed's Hill. *Embrasures* are openings in the rampart through which cannon were fired; a *platform* was a flooring of strong planks laid on the ground to support heavy guns. It often was sloped to minimize their recoil. See *Military Collector and Historian*, Summer, 1968, 46-49 for their general appearance.

(7) *MHSP*, XIV, 85-86

(8) *Dawson,* 437. This is from material collected by Prescott's descendents and so may be somewhat exaggerated.

(9) *MHS. Peter Brown's Letter.* Rumors of treachery were so numerous that the Provincial Congress named a committee to inquire into them. It found no evidence to justify these rumors. A New Englander normally had rum handy, but few of them cared for it straight on a warm, dusty morning. Their usual on-the-job tipple was cider, beer, or switchel.

(10) *Banquettes* ". . a kind of step . . for the troops to stand upon, in order to fire over the parapet; it is . . . about 3 feet broad, and 4½ feet lower than the parapet." (*James*, 247)

(11) Colonel Gridley may have had something to do with this, if he did go back to Cambridge in the early morning. The time of Callender's departure and of his arrival at Breed's Hill are most uncertain.

CHAPTER X
GO AND OPPOSE THEM

(1) Graves had "shifted his flag" to the *Preston*, probably because of the *Somerset's* leaky condition. "Arming" the boats meant mounting a light gun (seldom more than a 3-pounder) at their bow to provide assault fire as the landing force came in to the beach. Occasionally they also might mount one or more swivels—small cannon or oversized muskets, throwing shot of less than 1-pound weight—along their sides.

(2) *MHSP*, XIV, 287.

(3) *Ward*, I, 84. As here, the number of boats usually is given as twenty-eight; Peter Brown thought ". . as many as 40." According to *Ward* "In each of the two leading boats were six brass fieldpieces," which seems contrary to all normal amphibious tactics, especially when the landing might be opposed. Howe himself said that the artillery came with the second wave. Probably the leading boats were from warships (as would be logical because of their better training and discipline) and so were armed—an unenlightened observer would confuse their boat guns with field-pieces.

(4) *Dawson*, 367.

(5) It is impossible to give the exact times such orders were given or received. The disposition of regiments used here is largely from *Martyn*, modified according to after-action reports, court-martial proceedings, and personal accounts, but it is little better than an educated guess. Stark—and apparently Little, Woodbridge, and Doolittle—already had sent some men to support Prescott.

(6) *Force*, 4, II, 1029.

(7) *Coffin*, 376-377.

(8) Ford, Worthington C. (Ed.) *Correspondence and Journals of Samuel B. Webb*, 3 Vols., New York, 1893, I, 64-65. Chester's opinion of Massachusetts officers agreed heartily with Washington's and Charles Lee's.

(9) Another account says they were given chunks of lead cut from the pipes of a Cambridge church organ. Dearborn served creditably throughout the Revolution, but did not write his memoirs until 1818, by which time his memories may have been considerably self-edited. Obviously, however, Stark did have to issue ammunition—but it is not clear whether this was all his men had, or that it was to bring them up to the thirty rounds supposedly normal in Ward's army.

(10) The perambulations of Gridley's and Callender's artillery companies are impossible to untangle. Prescott's account is not clear; Peter Brown said there were four guns at the redoubt, but mentioned only one captain. It seems likely that both companies left the redoubt and that Gridley returned under duress, but that he and his men soon abandoned their guns.

(11) *Force*, 4, II, 1438.

(12) Stocking, Rev. C.H.W. *The History and Genealogy of the Knowltons of England and America*, 1897.

(13) *Dawson*, 386. *Geo. III Corr.*, 3:221.

(14) Lt. Col. John Robinson and Major Henry Wood of Prescott's Regiment. Possibly one went into Charlestown, the other into the area between the breastwork and the Rail Fence.

(15) Brown's estimate seems reasonable for the men he could see—those in the redoubt/breastwork area. Because of the configuration of the ground and the distance, he could not have had any clear idea of the forces at the Rail Fence or in Charlestown.

(16) See the much-amended final draft in *MHS*. The Americans were anxious to publicize the burning of Charlestown as a major British atrocity and so tinkered judiciously with the facts.

(17) *Dawson*, 402 ff.

(18) *Heath*, 3.

(19) *Dawson*, 422.

CHAPTER XI
IF HE WISHED THE PLACE BURNED

(1) From Howe's letter, 22 June '75, to his brother, Lord Howe.

(2) *Dawson*, 375, 380, for American reports of their presence. *Barker*, 148, notes the presence of three gondolas there on the 18th. It is not certain that these craft were fitted with masts and sails. Howe certainly wanted them completely overhauled.

(3) *Williams*, 18. Mauduit, Israel. *Three Letters to Lord Viscount Howe, with Remarks on the Attack at Bunker Hill*, London, 1781, 39. After the battle it was noted that these fences were studded with bullets ". . not a hand's breadth from each other."

(4) *Coffin*, 370. Unfortunately, this description of Stark's activities comes through James Wilkinson, whose veracity is thoroughly questionable. Wilkinson claimed to have walked over the battlefield with Stark after the British evacuated Boston in 1776. His description of the terrain at least is accurate.

(5) Frothington, Richard. *Command in the Battle of Bunker Hill*, Boston, 1850, 10. A schooner big enough to carry 500-600 men would have been an abnormally large vessel. This report raises the suspicion that Sargent had enjoyed the old New England custom of flip for breakfast. The confusion his report caused suggests what Gage might have accomplished by a well-staged feint.

(6) *Dawson*, 400-402. Whitcomb had not yet received his formal commission as major general, but—like Warren and Pomeroy—was accepted as a general officer. There is confusion over the two Whit-combs then with the army—General John Whitcomb and Colonel Asa Whitcomb who commanded one of the Massachusetts regiments.

(7) *Dawson*, 367.

(8) *Pomeroy*, 164. *Heath*, 13-14. Why Pomeroy went to the Rail Fence can only be guessed—he would have been weary, and it was the closest position.

(9) *Drake*, 18.

(10) *Coffin*, 369.

(11) *Force*, 4, II, 1438.

(12) *MHS*, *New Hampshire Revolutionary Papers*, I, 301.

(13) Three eyewitness estimates were: *Rawdon* "above 6,000"; *Kemble*, at least 4,000; Howe, "near 6,000, but I do not suppose that they had more than between 4,000 and 5,000 engaged." Though the British might tend to exaggerate the American strength for propaganda purposes, many of their officers were reliable eyewitnesses, and used to estimating the strength of a distant body of troops.

(14) The tide being at its heighth, this would be possible and would save time since these units were to be on the left wing of Howe's attack.

(15) *Graves*, I, 117-118.

(16) *Fonblanque*, 155.

CHAPTER XII
A MOMENT THAT I NEVER FELT BEFORE

(1) There *were* three attacks, but each was launched against a different part of the American position, and all of them included attempts to envelop one of its flanks. All students of this battle should read Murdock, Harold, *Bunker Hill: Notes and Queries on a*

Famous Battle, Boston, 1927—an outstanding example of incisive historical analysis.

(2) *De Berniere's Map*: the light infantry companies seem to have been, from front to rear, those of the 23d, 4th, 10th, 52d, 43d, 65th, 59th, 47th, 35th, 38th, and 5th.

(3) *Ibid*.

(4) *MHS*.

(5) *Coffin*, 370, 377-387. An example of what would happen when the defending force was too weak occurred in 1777 when Clinton took Fort Montgomery and Fort Clinton on the Hudson. These were strong, carefully built fortifications mounting heavy guns and protected by an abatis, but weakly garrisoned; the Americans stood firm and shot straight. Though Clinton had no artillery, the British carried both forts with the bayonet at first rush. (*Ward*, II, 519.) For this reason, Prescott's claim that he had only 150 men in the redoubt is highly dubious.

(6) The misadventures of these guns are almost as murky as those of their American opposite numbers, so that it is difficult to coordinate them with the various British attacks.

(7) In this case, each company would fire in turn from one flank to the other. However, Howe's account, which follows, was written at the time and must be more accurate than Dearborn's aging memories.

(8) *Geo. III Corr.*, 3:222. Some writers have attributed this description to the repulse of Howe's second attack, which may be correct. This, however, was the first repulse Howe had experienced and so the remark seems to me to fit this first attack better. Howe was an awkward hand at expressing himself in writing.

(9) *Frothingham*, 415-416. There is the possibility, of course, that Dana was not so much frightened as an undisciplined wisenheimer who had heard that it was advisable to get the enemy to fire first. *MHS, Elijah Hide* (See Chapter XV) says Knowlton ordered his men not to fire ". . until the enemy were got within fifteen rods, and then not until the word was given."

(10) I have been unable to find any mention of the pioneers during the battle; probably they were left in Boston with Cleaveland (See Chapter VII).

(11) *Coffin*, 370. It is possible that Prescott's statement relates in whole or part to the beginning of Pigot's first actual attack.

(12) *Dawson*, 367. This is by an unidentified "British officer in Boston," written 5 July 1775: Unlike most of the anonymous letters concerning this battle, this one has an authentic "field soldier" smell to it.

(13) *Drake*, 27-28.

(14) *Coffin*, 377-387. The coats of British officers, made of better cloth than the privates', usually were much brighter—scarlet, instead of red. The same was true of sergeants' uniforms, to a lesser degree.

(15) *Dawson*, 367.

(16) *Ibid*. Grapeshot might be used to prepare an attack or cover a withdrawal, but its "spread" made it dangerous to use in support of attacking troops.

(17) *Dawson*, 368. *Lister*, 66. See also Stedman, Charles, *The History of the Origin, Progress, and Termination of the American War*, London, 1794, 129, for a contemporary Loyalist's view. Cleaveland's alibi—a letter written on 3 December to Lord Amherst is in the British Museum. There would have been nothing to plunder on the uninhabited northern side of the Charlestown Peninsula; all of the 6-pounders reportedly were out of action; and the number of rounds sent would be of little importance if many of them were of the wrong caliber.

CHAPTER XIII
TO GET AT THE LIVING

(1) Stacey, C. P. *Quebec, 1759*, Toronto, 1959, 3.

(2) *De Berniere's Map. Drake*, 27-28. This is another episode which is impossible to time exactly. It probably happened as described here, after Pigot's first attack; possibly it came slightly later during his second and final one. Adjutant Waller of the Marines describes driving the enemy from ". . the natural defenses of the redoubt . . . climbing over rails and hedges . . ." just before the last attack.

(3) Clinton's busy-busy description makes it plain that there yet were some Americans lurking along the southern and eastern edges of Charlestown, either unable to withdraw through the burning town or too fighting-mad to consider retreating. Burgoyne's version—more florid but less excited—mentions that he and Clinton had seen two regiments sent to reinforce Howe ". . on the beach, seeming in embarrassment which way to march." Whether this was part of the 47th and 1st Marines, or merely a gathering of walking wounded, is unknown.

(4) This liquid is variously given as "rum" or "beer." The reproduction in *Martyn* shows a squiggle that could be either.

(5) *Dawson*, 387. Captain Chester's letter has been much copied and quoted. Though the general sense always is the same, there are differences in the wording.

(6) *Dawson*, 400-402.

(7) Febiger was a former Danish officer who had come to America a few years previously. Affectionately known as "Old Denmark," he was a thorough soldier who served with distinction throughout the Revolution, ending as Colonel of the 2d Virginia Regiment of the Continental Line.

(8) This lull probably lasted less than half an hour. Some participants hardly noticed it.

(9) *Force*, 4, II, 1098. This shows 2 captains, one lieutenant, one sergeant, and 8 rank-and-file. Cleaveland reported 13 wounded, one of them fatally, which agrees with the above, if the artillery officer on Howe's staff is added. Casualties among the attached infantrymen are not mentioned.

(10) Only the general direction of this final attack is certain: the regimental objectives have been worked out by deduction. Since Howe's division had suffered very heavy casualties, its units would cover only a narrow front even when deployed into one line.

(11) Either its home-made carriage broke down, or British artillery fire wrecked it.

(12) The traditional story is that the redoubt fell only because Prescott's men ran out of ammunition. Prescott wrote ". . Our ammunition being nearly exhausted, could keep up only a scattering fire." Peter Brown, who was in the redoubt with him, says nothing about an ammunition shortage; Boynton, who also was there, put it ". . we began a hot fire for a short time. The enemy scaling our walls . . . we was ordered to retreat." Both Waller and Rawdon make it plain that the Americans still were doing a lot of shooting when the British actually broke into the redoubt. While the Americans undoubtedly had used up most of their ammunition, it was the fact that the British were about to surround the redoubt that made it untenable.

(13) *Drake*, 28. *Adm.*, 1:486. The second paragraph here precedes the first in Waller's actual report; I have shifted it to maintain the sequence. Pitcairn was mortally wounded, not killed as Waller thought.

(14) *Dawson*, 390.

(15) This is the commonly accepted version. Some Americans even invented a noble death statement for him. By contrast, there is Dearborn's story of seeing Warren's dead body under a tree behind the redoubt, just after the repulse of Pigot's first attack. Warren's conspicuous clothing would have made him a shining mark.

CHAPTER XIV
A POOR STONE FENCE

(1) Clinton's reasons for putting this into cipher probably existed only in his sometimes peculiar mind. Other officers were as frank in open correspondence.

(2) This, and the next few lines are from notes Clinton wrote in 1785. Such inflated claims are not uncommon with Clinton; they cast doubt on many of his other unsupported assertions—such as that (see Chapter VII) he detected the Americans occupying the Charlestown Peninsula on the night of 16 June. A letter Clinton wrote on 23 June 1775 was far less pretentious: "The Hopes of being of a little service where I thought I saw an opportunity brought me to the assistance of my friend Gen. Howe *en volontaire*: the affair however was in great measure decided on my getting there, and I had little more to do than offer my assistance and advice wherever it could be of use."

(3) *Dawson*, 439. Other accounts suggest that Gardiner had only three or four of his companies with him. The actual sequence here cannot be verified through available references.

(4) *MHSP*, XIV, 62.

(5) *Wade*, 19-22. The Committee of Safety's official report granted that ". . . this party of the ministerial troops evidenced a courage worthy of a better cause." Warner's company was especially hard hit; Little's total loss being only seven killed and twenty-three wounded. By comparison, Dearborn's company of Stark's Regiment, fighting from behind the Rail Fence, had only one man killed and five wounded.

(6) *Dawson*, 400-402.

(7) *Wade*, 21.

(8) Accusation by Capt. Luke Drury, 4 Oct. 75—from an original document kindly furnished by Mr. William Guthman.

(9) *Coffin*, 386-387.

(10) *MHSP*, XIV, 85-86.

(11) *Dawson*, 438. The story is from the "Prescott Manuscript" and may be apocryphal.

(12) *Journal of the Society for Army Historical Research*, 1974, 188.

(13) *Fonblanque*, 154.

CHAPTER XV
BUT WANT OFFICERS

(1) The British advanced sometime after 3:00 PM; the battle ended at 5:00 PM. Prescott wrote that ". . We kept the fort about one hour and twenty minutes after the attack with small arms [Pigot's initial feint]."

(2) *Force*, 4, II, 1079, 1098-1099. *Dawson*, 361.

(3) See Appendix I: American Infantry Weapons.

(4) *Force*, 4, II, 1029, 1328. American casualties included personnel from 19 regiments: *Massachusetts*—Prescott, Frye, Bridge, Jonathan Brewer, Nixon, Little, Doolittle, Woodbridge, Gerrish, Whitcomb, Gardner, Ward, Scammon, and Gridley. (Peter Brown said Prescott's lost "37 killed, 4 or 5 taken captive, about forty-seven wounded.) *New Hampshire*—Stark, Reed, and Sargent. *Connecticut*—Spencer and Putnam. In addition, there were some casualties identified as "militia," "minute men," and "volunteers." *Frothingham*, 193, has a listing—probably incomplete—of casualties by regiments. One contemporary letter gives Connecticut losses as 13 "missing" (dead or prisoners) and 23 wounded. Graves said that 40 Americans were found buried on Bunker's Hill; Gage reported burying "near 100 more" on the 18th, and confirmed the figure of 30 prisoners.

(5) *Force*, 4, II, 1029, 1097.

(6) *Barker*, 145. Loring, of course, was the husband of the beautiful Mrs. Loring who became Howe's mistress—to Joshua Loring's great profit. Gage had made him sheriff in compensation for property the Americans had confiscated. Gage's reasons for appointing Cunningham are not apparent.

(7) *Barker*, 148-149.

(8) Rumors of this period are entertainingly covered in Abigail Adams' letters. See Adams, Charles F. *Familiar Letters of John Adams and His Wife Abigail Adams During the Revolution*, New York, 1876.

(9) *Barker*, 149-150. *Williams*, 20. *Kemble*, 44. The "Block House" was a British battery in south Boston near the Boston Neck. Its guns could not stop Washington's occupation of the peninsula in March 1776.

(10) *Barker*, 150.

(11) *New England Quarterly*, Sept., 1952, 367. Warren's body was exhumed after the British evacuated Boston. Paul Revere is supposed to have identified it by two false teeth he had made for Warren.

(12) *Barker*, 148-151. This includes excerpts from Howe's Orderly Book.

(13) *Force*, 4, II, 1097-1098. *French*, 258-259. *Gage Corr*. II, 686-687. *C.O.*, Class 5/121.

(14) *Dawson*, 364-365, 368, 381. *Kemble*, 44. *Rawdon*.

(15) *MHS Force*, 4, II, 1018-1019.

(16) *MHS* has a copy of the original document, showing how the authors labored over their wording. Thacher also began the fable of the British retreating to their boats at Moulton's Point after each repulse.

(17) *Colonial Society of Massachusetts, Transactions*, 1933-1937, XXXII, 262-273. (See also Murdock's chapter on Martin.)

(18) *Dawson*, 360. Needless to say, all of these stories still are used by some writers.

(19) *Freeman*, IV, 55.

(20) *Geo. III Corr.*, 1794. *Gage Corr.*, II, 206. The command in Canada went to General Guy Carleton.

(21) *Freeman*, 509-510.

(22) *New Hampshire State Papers*, VII, 526. *Martyn*, 108.

(23) *Dawson*, 376-378. More troops from Rhode Island and Connecticut had reinforced Ward.

(24) *Wade*, 27-33.

* * *

WEAPONS

By modern standards, the weapons used at Bunker Hill were both short-ranged and inaccurate. Properly employed, however, they were extremely effective man-killers. All firearms used black powder ammunition, which produced vast amounts of smoke.

BRITISH INFANTRY WEAPONS:

The standard British infantry weapon was the so-called "Brown Bess"—a smoothbore, muzzle-loading, flintlock musket, caliber .75, with a 42-inch barrel and an iron ramrod. Its bayonet had a 16-inch blade. Light infantry and artillerymen were issued a shorter, lighter musket of the same caliber. (A few of Gage's regiments carried a heavier, longer, older model, with a wooden ramrod. These were replaced at Halifax the next spring.)

The Brown Bess's maximum range was approximately 1,000 yards, but its *effective* range against individual targets was only 50 to 80 yards. Against troops in formation, it was effective up to some 200 yards. Its rate of fire (for well-trained troops with clean muskets) was 4 rounds a minute; this fell off as muskets became fouled from firing. Brown Bess's bullet had a devastating shock effect, possibly the greatest of any military weapon used in North America. As of 22 April 1775, all British troops in Boston were "to be completed to 60 rounds (of musket ammunition) per man."

Officers had swords, of varying regimental patterns, but normally with straight, single-edged, cut-and-thrust blades. In some regiments they also carried spontoons, but grenadier and light infantry officers frequently were equipped with fusils (light muskets, like the artillery model, but better made).

Sergeants, grenadiers, and drummers had short cutting swords; light infantrymen might have tomahawks. Grenadier and light infantry sergeants usually were armed with fusils; sergeants of battalion companies traditionally carried halberds, but there was a tendency to replace these with muskets or fusils. In the Royal Welch Fusiliers (the 23d Foot), for example, all officers and sergeants had fusils.

AMERICAN INFANTRY WEAPONS:

At this period, American infantry weapons were largely the personal arms brought in by volunteers, supplemented with whatever weapons their colony could scrape up from all possible sources. All were smoothbore, muzzle-loading flintlocks; popular legends aside, it is unlikely that any American at Bunker Hill carried a rifle—which at that time was a frontiersman's specialized weapon. Most American muskets were of types useful for both hunting and militia service. Their caliber ranged from the "bastard musket bore" of .69 to .75. They normally were were not equipped with gun slings or bayonets. Many had the old-style wooden ramrods, which might break in the stress of loading a fouled musket.

American weapons included numbers of the older, more cumbersome types of British military muskets. There were some French and Spanish weapons, captured in the colonial wars, and a sprinkling of very long-barreled fowling pieces. This assortment of types and calibers made ammunition supply difficult: soldiers often had to prepare their own and might use anything available. After Bunker Hill, a British surgeon noted "The Provincials had either exhausted their ball, or they were determined that every wound should prove fatal; their muskets were charged with old nails and angular pieces of iron . . ." Because of the shortage of gunpowder in New England, American soldiers seldom were issued more than 30 cartridges.

Although New England militia laws required each citizen to have either a sword or a hatchet, in addition to his musket, few American enlisted men at Bunker Hill seem to have carried either. Also, comparatively few of them possessed bayonets—only Colonel Little's regiment was reported as having a considerable number (382 for 509 officers and men) of them.

American officers carried a variety of swords, some of them crude weapons made by local blacksmiths. Most of them also had muskets or fusils.

ARTILLERY:

Artillery of this period was smoothbore and muzzle-loading. Cannon might be either bronze (usually termed "brass") or iron, the former being considered the more satisfactory material for field artillery. *Effective* ranges were approximately:

CALIBER	SOLID SHOT	GRAPESHOT
3 or 4-pounder gun	800 yards	400 yards
6-pounder gun	800 yards	500 yards
12-pounder gun	900 yards	600 yards
8-inch howitzer	900 yards (explosive shell)	500 yards

The maximum range of all calibers was considerably greater than the above effective ranges. Therefore a solid shot that had missed its target still could be dangerous to troops farther to the rear—such a shot might roll and bounce for hundreds of yards with enough momentum to kill or cripple anyone in its way. *Guns* had a comparatively flat trajectory; *howitzers* were designed for high-angle fire so that they could drop explosive shells behind enemy entrenchments.

COMMON TYPES OF AMMUNITION

Solid shot, a solid iron ball, was employed against troops in formation, palisades, and light masonry buildings. It was not effective against solidly built breastworks.

Explosive shell, a hollow iron ball, filled with a bursting charge of black powder, also was used against troops and buildings, and had a limited incendiary effect. At this time, explosive shell was fired only from howitzers and mortars. Its fuzes often burned erratically, causing the shell to explode too soon, or going out in flight.

Grapeshot, a number of small iron balls contained in a heavy canvas bag, and corded together to form a cylinder to fit the bore of a gun, was used for short-range fire against troops. When fired the balls "spread," like shotgun ammunition.

Canister, a cylindrical container of small iron balls (smaller than grapeshot), was highly effective against troops at short range. It produced a denser "spread" than grapeshot, but had a somewhat shorter effective range.

Langrage was an improvised type of ammunition, made up of small pieces of scrap metal. The Massachusetts artillery regiment apparently employed it as a substitute for canister (On 18 April each of that regiment's twelve guns was to be provided with ". . thirty-three rounds of round shot, thirty-three rounds of grape shot, and thirty-three canisters of langrage . . . together with one hundred cartridges of powder.")

NAVAL ARTILLERY:

The 18 and 24-pounder guns carried by the larger British warships had effective ranges of over 1,200 yards. However, British naval gunnery was not accurate at such distances, the accepted naval tactic being to overwhelm an enemy with rapid, point-blank broadsides—often at less than 100 yards range. Consequently neither guns nor gunners were particularly dangerous to entrenched infantry a few hundred yards inland.

INCENDIARY AMMUNITION:

This was employed by both army and naval artillery for such missions as the burning of Charlestown. It included both "hot shot" and "carcasses." The first was ordinary solid shot, heated in a furnace until red hot. Great care was required in preparing and firing it. The carcass was a special shell with several vents, filled with pitch, gunpowder, tallow, and other combustibles: these took fire when the gun was discharged, and burned fiercely for several minutes.

APPENDIX II

WARSHIPS IN BOSTON HARBOR, 16-17 JUNE 1775. (1)

Boyne	70 guns (2)
Somerset	64 guns (2)
Preston	50 guns (2)
Glasgow	20 guns (3)
Lively	20 guns (3)
Falcon	14 guns (3)
Spitfire	6 guns (3-pounders) (4)

These Royal Navy ships were supplemented by the following Army-controlled vessels:
Symmetry 18 guns (9-pounders).
Gondolas - described by Graves as "2 Scows with a 12-pounder in each end."
The 40-gun frigate *Cerberus* was anchored in Nantasket Roads in the outer harbor, ready to sail for England with dispatches. She was not part of Graves' squadron and was not engaged.

(1) Reference: Graves' *Conduct.* It must be kept in mind that a warship of this period could use only one broadside—half of her guns—against a single target. Thus the *Glasgow*, for example, would never have more than 10 guns in action at once; the total number of ships' guns in action probably did not exceed 41.
(2) Not actively engaged.
(3) A 20-gun ship normally was armed with 9-pounder guns; sloops, such as the *Falcon*, with 6-pounders. (Clowes, William L. *The Royal Navy, A History*, London, 1898.)
(4) A small tender, recently acquired for service in Boston harbor, not listed as a regularly commissioned warship.

APPENDIX III

MASSACHUSETTS ARMY, 17 JUNE 1775. (1)

Regiment (2) Colonel	No.	Date Certified (3)	Station	Privates 9 June
Gerrish, Samuel	25	19 May	Cambridge	421 (4)
Learned, Ebenezer	14	19 May	Roxbury	(5)
Read, Joseph (6)	6	20 May	Roxbury	
Scammon, James	13	24 May	Cambridge	396
Thomas, John	2	26 May	Roxbury	
Ward, Artemus	1	26 May	Cambridge	449
Gardner, Thomas	15	26 May	Cambridge	425
Patterson, John (6)	12	26 May	Cambridge	422
Prescott, William	9	26 May	Cambridge	456
Cotton, Theophilus	4	26 May	Roxbury	
Bridge, Ebenezer	11	26 May	Cambridge	315
Whitcomb, Asa	5	26 May	Cambridge	470
Frye, James (6)	10	26 May	Cambridge	493
Doolittle, Ephraim	18	26 May	Cambridge	308
Walker, Timothy	3	26 May	Roxbury	
Danielson, Timothy	8	26 May	Roxbury	
Mansfield, John	7	27 May	Cambridge	345
Fellows, John	17	29 May	Roxbury	
Nixon, John	16	2 June	Cambridge	224
Glover, John	23	7 June	Marblehead	
Heath, William	21	14 June	Roxbury	
Brewer, David	20	17 June	Roxbury	
Brewer, Jonathan	19	17 June	Cambridge	318
Woodbridge, Benj.	22	(7)	Cambridge	242
Little, Moses	24	(7)	Cambridge	400
Gridley, Richard	Art.	(7)	Cambridge & Roxbury	370

(1) Sources: Force 4, II, 814, 823-830, 1350-1351, 1413-1414, 1629-1630; Lincoln, 552-577; Frothingham 118n.
(2) Massachusetts regiments were to be numbered ". . according to the rank or age of the counties . . ." from which they came, but the numbers shown here were not used until after Bunker's Hill. In addition to the regiments shown here, there was Colonel Edmund Phinney's (26th) regiment, still being organized in Maine, and four independent companies for coast defense. They are presented here in order of their certification.
(3) Known strengths of regiments when certified are presented here in quotes, plus additional available information as follows: *Gerrish* "595 in camp." Regiment much reduced subsequently when six companies dropped out to join Little, seven companies on 22 June. *Read* "Officers, 30, Men 564." *Scammon* "35 Officers, 512 rank and file." *Thomas* "Officers and privates, 596." *Ward* "Officers and privates, 440." *Patterson* "28 officers, 496 enlisted men." *Prescott* "Officers and soldiers, 483." *Bridge* Apparently only six companies fully organized, 27 May. *Whitcomb* "I have a full regiment." *Frye* "Whole number, 556." *Doolittle* Only six companies fully organized, 12 June. *Walker* "Officers and privates, 562." *Danielson* Apparently only eight companies in early June. *Fellows* "Officers and soldiers, 548." *Nixon* ". . regiment is in good forwardness." Regiment almost broken up by internal difficulties—largely over choice of its field officers—in late May. Only six companies on 5 June, but three more organized by 16 June. *Glover* "Total number of men, 505 . . . about three quarters . . . armed with effective firelocks." *Heath* "Total rank and file, 466." *Brewer, David* ". . near five hundred men." Only nine companies on 17 June, only 307 men had weapons, 34 men enroute to join. *Brewer, Jonathan* "Total number . . . 371." Only eight companies on 17 June, only 302 men had weapons. *Woodbridge* ". . eight companies are in good forwardness." This regiment had been on duty since Lexington/Concord as a unit of "minute men." For some reason, the Committee of Safety was slow to issue Woodbridge beating orders to recruit volunteers. On 16 June, 354 officers and men; only 273 men had muskets. *Little* "Total number . . . 582." On 15 June, 509 officers and men in eight companies, all armed, 382 had bayonets, one company detached to Cape Ann. *Gridley* Strength on 16 June, 427. A large part of their arms declared unfit

51

for service.

(4) Total of this return for regiments around Cambridge on 9 June was given as 6,063 privates, 1,581 NCOs and drummers.

(5) On 9 June, the regiments around Roxbury had 3,992 privates in 93 companies.

(6) These names often appear on official returns as Reed, Paterson and Fry.

(7) Certified after Bunker's Hill.

NEW HAMPSHIRE ARMY,
17 JUNE 1775. (1)

COLONEL	NO.	STATION	STRENGTH
Stark, John	1	Medford	750 rank-and-file (5)
Poor, Enoch (2)	2	New Hampshire	
Reed, James (3)	3	Just west of Charlestown Neck	486 rank-and-file (5)
Sargent, Paul D. (4)		Lechmere's Point	220 (estimate)

(1) Stark had an oversized regiment of 13 companies; Reed had only 8, the New Hampshire Committee of Safety having decided that ".. the other two companies . . . be taken out of Col. Stark's Regiment." They still were with Stark on 17 June. (*NHHS,* VII, 3.)

(2) Poor's Regiment (approximately 600) did not leave New Hampshire until after 17 June.

(3) Spelled variously "Reed," "Reid," and "Read" in official documents.

(4) Sargent had four organized companies, and two or three incomplete ones slowly recruiting in New Hampshire. On 9 June the Massachusetts Committee of Safety had recommended that these companies be discharged from the Massachusetts service, so as to enter that of New Hampshire. (*Force,* 5, II, 1349-1350.)

(5) Return of 14 June. A good many men in both regiments seem to have lacked weapons. (*Bouton,* VII, 474.)

CONNECTICUT ARMY,
17 JUNE 1775. (1) (4)

COLONEL	NO. STATION	STRENGTH
Wooster, David	1 New York area (2)	
Spencer, Joseph	2 Roxbury/Cambridge	1,000
Putnam, Israel	3 Cambridge	1,000
Hinman, Benjamin	4 Ticonderoga	
Waterbury, David	5 New York area	
Parsons, Samuel H.	6 New London/ Cambridge	200 (3)

(1) *Force,* 4, II, 414-417.

(2) Two companies sent to New London, Ct. on 17 June. (*Records of Connecticut,* XV, 87-89.)

(3) Two companies ordered to Boston on 7 June. The rest of the regiment was dispatched on the 17th. (*Records of Connecticut,* XV, 85, 87-89.)

(4) There also was an "Independent and Ranging Company" of 28 officers and men, commanded by Captain Peter Perret (whose name has a strange variety of misspellings), engaged in reconnaissance missions around Boston. (*Connecticut Records,* XV, 88.) It apparently served on 17 June.

RHODE ISLAND ARMY,
17 JUNE 1775. (1)

COLONEL	STATION	STRENGTH
Church, Thomas	Roxbury	500
Hitchcock, Daniel	Roxbury	500
Varnum, James M.	Roxbury	(2)

(1) These regiments were not numbered. They were sent forward to Boston by companies, as organized. One regiment included a company of artillery.

(2) As of 2 June no elements of this regiment had reached Roxbury, but by 17 June there were 1,390 Rhode Island troops there. (*Force,* 4, II, 893, 1143 ff and 1152 ff.)

APPENDIX IV

BRITISH TROOPS IN BOSTON

In 1763 the peace-time strength of a regiment of Foot had been set at 423 privates per regiment (*W.O.* 4/987). Of these, however, some 20 probably were "contingent men"—non-existent soldiers whose pay the companies drew to cover hospital expenses, repairs to weapons and accouterments, funerals, and similar expenses (*W.O.* 1/980, f 265). Most British regiments never achieved this figure.

The approximate strength of the regiments in Boston can be determined from company muster rolls, commissary tables, and various order books and journals. Usually those deal only with "effective" strengths (a most illusive term) and with the "rank-and-file" (usually privates and corporals). There also were occasional major "states," showing the entire strength and disposition of the force, and the researcher can attempt to work backward or forward from these. Many of these documents now are missing, and very few are complete or accurate in the modern sense—the 18th century was not possessed by a desire for exact statistics.

The following are examples of this computation of regimental strength:

4th Foot - Five companies were mustered in January 1775. Each had 2 sergeants, 2 or 3 corporals, and (respectively) 25, 29, 26, 28, and 26 privates. Four of the companies had drummers. The approximate regimental strength therefore would be 326 enlisted men. On 12 March Mackenzie lists it as having 315 effective rank-and-file.

23d Foot - When mustered in January, each of its companies had 2 sergeants, 2 or 3 corporals, one drummer, and an average of 26 privates for an approximate 315 enlisted men. In March, Mackenzie recorded 314 rank-and-file; after Lexington/Concord he showed 303 enlisted men, including 49 in the hospital.

49th Foot - Each company had an average of 6 NCOs, one drummer, and 38 privates for an approximate total of 450 enlisted men.

59th Foot - Mustered with an average company strength of one sergeant, 2 corporals, one drummer, and some 19 privates, giving it an approximate 230 enlisted men.

64th Foot - Commissary tables show an average company enlisted strength of 42, which would mean an unusually strong regiment of 420 men. However, another source shows only 374.

Since the number of men in the hospital, or detailed as officers' servants is unknown, and the portion of the 35th and 49th Foot ashore and available for duty is uncertain, an exact head count of Gage's strength on 17 June 1775 is impossible. The following table is therefore approximate; where possible casualties from Lexington/Concord have been applied.

Unit	Effective Rank-and-File	Source	Portion Engaged
4th Foot	290	W.O. 12/2194; Mackenzie	Flank companies
5th Foot	300	Estimate	Entire regiment
10th Foot	360	W.O. 12/2750	Flank companies
23d Foot	280	W.O. 12/3960; Mackenzie	Flank companies
35th Foot	450 (1)	Based on 49th Foot muster	Flank companies
38th Foot	300	Estimate	Entire regiment
43d Foot	300	Estimate	Entire regiment
47th Foot	280	Mackenzie	Entire regiment
49th Foot	450 (1)	W.O. 12/6032	Not engaged
52d Foot	300	Estimate	Entire regiment
59th Foot	230	W.O. 12/6786	Flank companies
63d Foot	450	Based on 49th Foot muster	Flank companies (2)
64th Foot	420 (?)	Commissary tables	Not engaged
"Incorporated Corps"	270	Estimate	Flank companies
Total Infantry	4,680 (3)		
Marines	1,000	Mackenzie. C.O., Class 5/92	Both battalions (2)
17th Light Dragoons	196	Embarkation roster	Not engaged
Recruits 4 Companies	422	Gage	Not engaged
Artillery	144	Estimate	Elements
Total	6,442		

Note that the above regimental strengths include the flank companies (grenadiers and light infantry) which actually—except for those of the 64th Foot which were with their regiment at Castle William, and the 49th Foot which apparently had not yet disembarked—had been detached and grouped into provisional battalions. These flank companies were supposed to be kept at 39 rank-and-file, plus 2 or 3 sergeants and a drummer. All companies normally had 2 or 3 officers; some battalion companies seem to have had only one available for duty.

As an *approximate* computation of the combat strength of a typical regiment on 17 June, take the 47th Foot:

Effective rank-and-file	280
Sergeants present	28 (4)
Drummers present	13 (4)
Officers Present	21 (4) (5)
Total	342
Men sick, confined, on furlough or detached service	− 49 (4)
	293
Detached flank companies, officers and men	− 90
	203
Pioneers, assigned to Artillery commander	− 3
	200
Camp guard left in Boston	− 24 (6)
	176
Lieutenant colonel, major, adjutant	− 3
Officers and men in 8 battalion companies	173

A battalion company therefore probably had one or 2 officers, 2 or 3 sergeants, a drummer, and 16 or 17 corporals and privates. This high proportion of officers and NCOs undoubtedly was one of the reasons for the extraordinary steadiness the British displayed.

(1) Not all landed 17 June.
(2) The battalion companies of the 63d Foot and 2d Marine Battalion were not actually engaged, having landed too late to take part in the last attack.
(3) This total probably includes the 180 infantrymen temporarily assigned to the artillery.
(4) Typical figures, taken from a "state" of this regiment on 17 March 1776 (W.O. 36/3).
(5) This includes the lieutenant colonel (colonel not present), major, adjutant, and company officers: the chaplain, quartermaster, surgeon, and surgeon's mate are omitted.
(6) "One Subaltern, one Serjeant, one Corporal, one Drummer, and twenty privates."

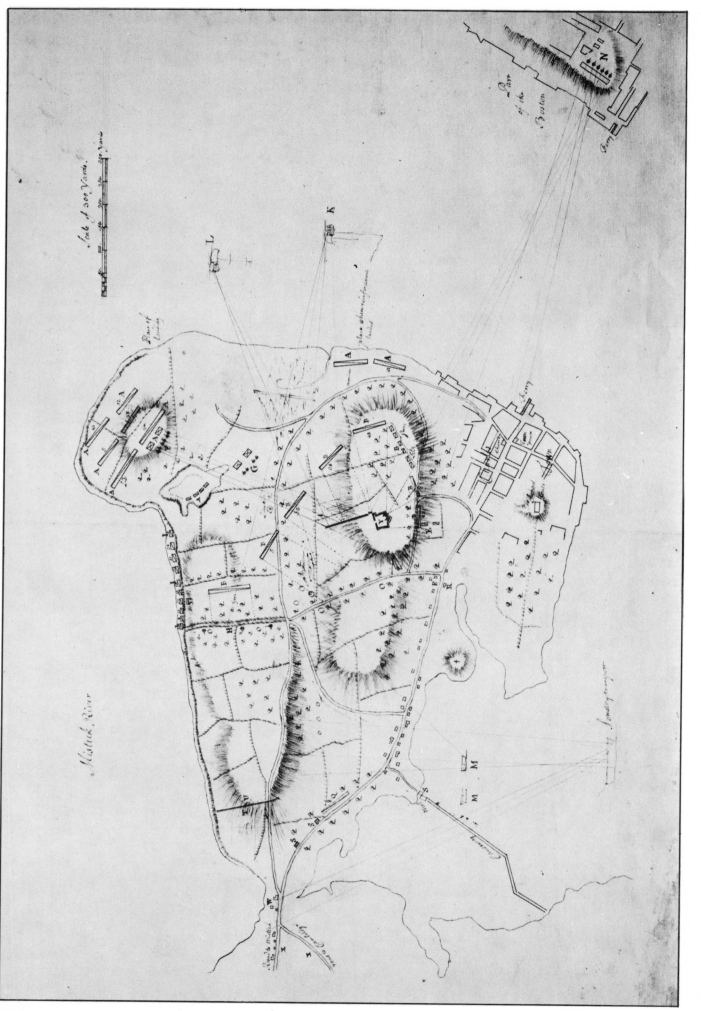

This map, although untitled and unsigned, is believed to be the lost original De Berniere map of the Battle of Bunker's Hill made by British Captain Henry De Berniere of the 10th Foot. (Geography and Map Division Library of Congress G3764.B6S3 1775 .B3 Vault.) This attribution, though inconclusive, is based on the fact that there are similarities between the handwriting on this map and the handwriting on the map of the Road from Roxbury to Concord, which is generally recognized as having been made by De Berniere. (G3764.B6P2 1772 .R6 Vault;

British Maps of the American Revolution 27/3) The map is oriented north and, as reduced, is at the scale of ½ inch to 100 yards. The original references to the map, which were undoubtedly numerous and possibly on a separate sheet, have been lost, and a few references, in a different hand, were later added to the map. The author has restored the original references as well as possible, and has rephrased some of them for greater clarity, on opposite page.

(A-A) First position of British troops after landing. Note separate landing sites of Howe's original force and of the reinforcements—47th Regiment and Marines. (B-B) Second position: Time not specified—apparently a combination of the first and the final attacks. (C-C) Apparently omitted. Another version of this map identifies it as "Ground on which the different Regiments marched to form the line." (D-D) Apparently omitted. Another version of this map identifies it as "Direction in which the attack was made upon the Redoubt and Breastwork." (E-E) Detachment from the 47th Regiment and the Marines "to silence the Fire from the Barn." Barn is represented by the left-hand E, at a road junction leading out of Charlestown. (F) Initial position of Howe's field artillery on Moulton's Hill. (G) Point in front of Moulton's Hill at which the 6-pounders were "stopt by the marsh" while advancing with the grenadiers in the first attack. (H) The Rail Fence ("Breastwork formed of Pickets, Hay, Stones etc..") and American artillery. The extension that Stark built across the beach is not shown. (I-I) "Light Infantry advancing along the shore to force the right [end] of the [Rail Fence] H." (K-L) "The *Lively* and *Falcon*, hauled close to the shore to rake the low ground before the troops advanced." The *Spitfire* is not shown. (M) Initial position of the gondolas, off southwest shore of Charlestown Peninsula. (N) Copp's Hill Battery in north Boston. (O) Americans: "The Rebels behind all the stone walls, trees and Brushwood etc. Their numbers uncertain having constantly large columns to reinforce them during the action." (P) Not shown. Another version of this map shows it with the symbols for the three *fleches,* with the remark, "Place from where the Grenadiers received a very heavy fire." Note that this map shows only a single *fleche,* at the northwest corner of the pond, directly in front of the 5th Regiment. (Q) Position of 52nd Regiment on the night of 17 June. (R) Position of 47th Regiment, night of 17 June. (S) Detachments holding the mill and two storehouses, night of 17 June. (T) Breastwork erected by the rest of Howe's force along the western slope of Bunker's Hill, night of 17 June. (U) References lost from original map. (W) Charlestown Neck. (X) Routes by which the American reinforcements advanced. (Y) American redoubt on Breed's Hill. Note that two cannon are shown in the redoubt. General Notes: "J" and "V" often were omitted from such reference lists because of the likelihood of confusing them with other letters, such as "I" and "U". The size of the warships is greatly exaggerated. The *Glasgow* apparently was anchored slightly to the west and south of the *Symmetry*. Note the numerous fence lines. The small isolated hill, marked with a cross, on the southern shore of the Charlestown Peninsula, may have been the site of the local cemetery. If so, the "Jews' burying ground" mentioned by Clinton probably was in this general area. The position of the American cannon along the Rail Fence probably is guesswork.

INDEX OF NAMES

A

Abercrombie, Lt. Col. James 18, 23, 24, 37
Abercromby, Maj. Gen. James 5, 10, 12
Adams, Samuel 19
Amherst, Maj. Gen. Jeffrey 5, 11, 18, 26

B

Barker, Lt. John 16, 17, 38
Barnes, Maj. Edward 29, 36
Bernierc, Lt. Henry de 16
Bishop, Capt. Thomas 21
Boynton, Thomas 24
Braddock, Maj. Gen. Edward 5, 16
Bradstreet, Col. John 5, 25
Brown, Sgt. Lemuel 26
Brewer, Col. Jonathan 11, 26, 29, 35
Brickett, Lt. Col. James 20, 25
Bridge, Col. Ebenezer 20, 25, 26, 29, 35
Brooks, Maj. John 25, 26
Brown, Pvt. Peter 24, 25, 26, 27, 30, 35
Browne, Capt. William 16
Buckmaster, Lt. Col. William 35
Burgoyne, Maj. Gen. John 3, 18, 19, 21, 22, 26, 30, 32, 36, 38
Butler, Adj. John 35

C

Callender, Capt. John 25, 27, 29, 40
Campbell, John (See Loudoun, Lord)
Chadds, Capt. 39
Chester, Capt. John 12, 26, 34, 36
Church, Dr. Benjamin 10, 16, 18, 20

Clark, Capt. James 36
Clarke, Lt. John 39
Cleaveland, Col. Samuel 15, 23, 31, 32
Clinton, Maj. Gen. Henry 3, 18, 21, 22, 23, 24, 28, 30, 32, 35, 36, 38, 39
Coit, Capt. William 36
Colden, Gov. Cadwallader 7
Collingwood, Midshipman Cuthbert 26
Cumberland, William Augustus, Duke of, 5
Cunningham, William 38

D

Dana, Lt. 31
Dartmouth, Lord (Legge, William) 6, 39
Dearborn, Capt. Henry 24, 26, 27, 31, 34, 35
Doolittle, Col. Ephraim 11, 25, 26, 29, 35
Dorchester, Lord 38
Dunmore, Gov. John 7, 8
Dutton, Lt. John 37

E

Estaing, Charles-Hector, Comte d' 3

F

Febiger, Adj. Christian 34
Folsom, Brig. Gen. Nathaniel 12
Frye, Col. James 20, 26, 29, 35

G

Gage, Lt. Gen. Thomas 3-8, 10, 13-26, 28, 32, 34, 36, 37, 38
Gardner, Col. Thomas 11, 26, 29, 34, 36, 37, 40

Gates, Brig. Gen. Horatio 40
George III 5, 7
Gerrish, Col. Samuel 11, 26, 29, 34, 36, 40
Glover, Col. John 11
Graves, Adm. Samuel 6, 7, 8, 10, 15, 18, 19-24, 26, 30, 32, 37, 38, 39
Graves, Lt. Thomas 18
Greene, Brig. Gen. Nathanael 3, 13, 19, 20
Gridley, Col. Richard 12, 19, 20, 21, 24, 25, 29, 40
Gridley, Capt. Samuel 12, 20, 24, 25, 26, 27, 40
Gridley, Maj. Scarborough 12, 29, 40
Gunning, Lt. Col. John 36

H

Hancock, John 19
Harris, Capt. George 16, 35
Heath, Brig. Gen. William 11, 12, 19, 20, 28
Hide, Elijah 39
Hodgkins, Lt. Joseph 36
Howe, Brig. Gen. George, 5
Howe, Maj. Gen. William 3, 10, 14, 18, 21, 22, 23, 27, 28, 30, 31, 32, 34, 35, 36, 37, 39
Huck, Dr. Richard 5
Hurley, Pvt. Martin 11

J

Jackson, Maj. Michael 36
James, Col. Thomas 24
Jones, Brig. Gen. Valentine 21

K

Kemble, Maj. Stephen 18, 38
Kittredge, Surg. Thomas 28
Knowlton, Capt. Thomas 20, 21, 27, 28, 29, 31, 40

L

Langdon, Rev. Samuel 20
Learned, Col. Ebenezer 11, 26
Lee, Arthur 39
Lee, Maj. Gen. Charles 25, 40
Legge, William (See Dartmouth Lord)
Lister, Lt. Jeremy 4
Little, Col. Moses 11, 24, 25, 29, 36, 40
Loring, Joshua 38
Loudoun, Lord (Campbell, John) 5
Lunt, Paul 3

M

McClary, Maj. Andrew 27, 37
McDonald, Pvt. John 14
Mackenzie, Lt. Frederick 15, 16
Mansfield, Col. John 24, 29, 34, 40
Martin, Rev. John 39
Martin, Gov. Josiah 8
Moore, Maj. Willard 35
Montresor, Col. James 16
Montresor, Lt. John 16, 28

N

Nesbitt, Lt. Col. William 35
Nixon, Col. John 11, 24, 26, 29, 35
Nutting, Capt. John 20, 21

P

Palmer, Col. Joseph 19
Parker, Lt. Col. Moses 35
Patterson, Col. John 11, 26, 34
Percy, Col. Hugh, Lord 4, 15, 21, 23, 24
Pigeon, Commissary, General John 10, 13
Pigot, Brig. Gen. Robert 21, 30, 31, 32, 34, 36
Pitcairn, Maj. John 15, 34, 35, 37
Pollard, Pvt. Asa 25
Pomeroy, Brig. Gen. Seth 11, 12, 20, 29, 35
Poor, Col. Enoch 12
Preble, Gen. Jedediah 10
Prescott, Col. William 20-28, 30-40
Prideaux, Col. John 5
Putnam, Brig. Gen. Israel 12, 17-21, 24-30, 34, 36, 37
Putnam, Capt. Israel Jr. 26

R

Rawdon, Lt. Francis (Lord Rawdon-Hastings) 23, 28, 35, 36
Reed, Col. James (also Ried and Read) 12, 17, 19, 21, 26, 27, 28, 38, 40
Robinson, Lt. Col. Lemuel 11, 27
Rogers, Maj. Robert 5, 11, 12, 18
Ruggles, Timothy 17

S

Sargent, Col. Paul 12, 29, 36
Scammon, Col. James 26, 29, 34, 36, 40
Smith, Capt. Joshia 26
Spencer, Brig. Gen. Joseph 12, 19, 20, 26
Stark, Col. John 3, 12, 17, 18, 19, 21, 24-31, 34, 35, 37, 38, 40
Steuben, Maj. Gen. Frederick von 24
Storrs, Lt. Col. Experience 24, 26, 37

T

Thatcher, Rev. Peter 24, 39
Thomas, Lt. Gen. John 11, 12, 17, 19, 23, 26, 38
Trevett, Capt. Samuel 29, 35, 40
Tudor, William 24, 25, 40

W

Wallace, Capt. James 7
Waller, Adj. John 35, 36, 37
Ward, Gen. Artemas 10-13, 16, 17, 19, 20, 23, 24-27, 29, 30, 34, 36-40
Ward, Joseph 34
Warner, Capt. Nathaniel 36
Warren, Maj. Gen. Joseph (Dr. Warren) 3, 11, 12, 20, 26, 29, 35, 38
Washington, Gen. George 4, 13, 39, 40
Wentworth, Gov. John 7
Whipple, Capt. Abraham 7
Whitcomb, Col. Asa 29, 34, 36
Whitcomb, Maj. Gen. John 11, 12, 29
White, Col. Benjamin 19
Williams, Lt. 14, 16, 38
Wolfe, Maj. Gen. James 5, 18, 26, 32
Woodbridge, Col. Benjamin 25, 26
Woods, Maj. Henry 27
Wyman, Lt. Col. Isaac 25, 27, 28